CAN
THE YUCATAN

Beach along the Riviera Maya © Randy Mayes/iStockphoto.com

Editorial Director Cynthia Clayton Ochterbeck

mustsees Cancún and the Yucatán

Editor	Jonathan P. Gilbert
Principal Writers	Jonathan P. Gilbert, Ellen Sarbone, Megan Smith
Production Manager	Natasha G. George
Cartography	GeoNova Publishing
Photo Editor	Alison Coupe, Yoshimi Kanazawa
Photo Research	Claudia Tate
Proofreaders	Alison Coupe, Rachel Mills
Layout	John Higginbottom, Natasha G. George
Cover & Interior Design	Chris Bell

Contact Us:

Michelin Maps and Guides
One Parkway South
Greenville, SC 29615
USA
www.michelintravel.com
michelin.guides@us.michelin.com

Michelin Maps and Guides
Hannay House
39 Clarendon Road
Watford, Herts WD17 1JA
UK
☎(01923) 205 240
www.ViaMichelin.com
travelpubsales@uk.michelin.com

Special Sales:

For information regarding bulk sales, customized
editions and premium sales, please contact
our Customer Service Departments:
USA   1-800-432-6277
UK   (01923) 205 240
Canada   1-800-361-8236

Michelin Apa Publications Ltd

A joint venture between Michelin and Langenscheidt

58 Borough High Street, London SE1 1XF, United Kingdom

No part of this publication may be reproduced in any form
without the prior permission of the publisher.

© 2009 Michelin Apa Publications Ltd
ISBN 978-1-906261-67-2
Printed: December 2008
Printed and bound: Himmer, Germany

Note to the reader:

Welcome to Cancún and the Yucatán

Mayan ruins overlooking the beach, Tulum

Introduction

Cancún and the Yucatán: Land of the Jaguar 28

p 30

p 54

p 96

p 136

TABLE OF CONTENTS

★★★ ATTRACTIONS

Unmissable historic, cultural and natural sights.

Beach, Cancún p 34

© Faby Vanyo/iStockphoto.com

Uxmal p 115

© Frédéric Soreau/Photononstop/Tips Images

Campeche p 97, 106

© Diana Bier/iStockphoto.com

© Dennis Sabo/iStockphoto.com

Isla Cozumel Reef   p 64

© Roberto A. Sanchez/iStockphoto.com

Xcaret   p 71

© Camhi Franck/Dreamstime.com

Cenote Dzitnup   p 105

© Bruce Herman/Mexico Tourism Board

Chichén Itzá   p 113

ACTIVITIES

Unmissable activities and entertainment

Cenote Diving   p 70, 104

© Alfredo Martinez/Mexico Tourism Board

Wave runners, Cancún   p 46

©Bruce Herman/Mexico Tourism Board

Sound and Light Show at
Chichén Itzá   p 113

© arturbo/iStockphoto.com

Mercado 28, Cancún   p 51

© Glowimages/Photoshot

Snorkeling, Cozumel   p 64

© Cozumel Promotion Board

MUST KNOW

©Bruce Herman/Mexico Tourism Board

Swimming with dolphins, Xcaret p 71

©Courtesy of OHL, El Camaleón, Mayakoba, Mexico

El Camaléon Golf p 87, 140

©Eduardo Fernandez/Elitours

Mangrove kayak p 46, 88–89

© Eric Nathan/Picture Colour Library

Nature Tours, Isla Contoy Bird Sanctuary p 41

STAR ATTRACTIONS

★★★ SIGHTS

Unmissable historic, cultural and natural sights

For more than 75 years people have used Michelin stars to take the guesswork out of travel. Our star-rating system helps you make the best decision on where to go, what to do, and what to see.

★★★	Unmissable
★★	Worth a trip
★	Worth a detour
No star	Recommended

ACTIVITIES

Unmissable activities, entertainment, restaurants and hotels

For every historic and natural sight in Cancún and the Yucatán there are a thousand more activities. We recommend all of the activities in this guide, but our top picks are highlighted with the Michelin Man logo.

Remember to look out for the Michelin Man for top activities.

IDEAS AND TOURS

Throughout this thematic guide you will find inspiration for a thousand different holidays in Cancún and the Yucatán. The following is a selection of ideas to start you off. The sites in **bold** are found in the index.

Weekend in Mérida★★

Settle into your hotel before hitting the streets for a weekend in Mérida. On Friday night have dinner and see a show at the **Universidad Autónoma de Yucatán**, where the performance of the **ballet folklórico** is spectacular. Spend your Saturday taking in the city's sites and museums by foot, but be sure to take your siesta before Mexican Night begins at the **Paseo Montejo**. On Sunday morning take coffee on the **Plaza Grande** and enjoy 'Mérida en Domingo,' before heading out of the city, north to pre-Hispanic **Dzibilchaltún** to revel in nature and history. Close the day with some bird watching after taking a swim in the site's cenote.

14-Day Trip

With two weeks for vacation and a sense of intrigue, spend a week at a **Playa del Carmen★★** Spanish school (*www.cancunspanish.com; www.cactuslanguage.com*). Here you can learn a bit of Spanish, visit **Isla Cozumel★★** and learn to scuba dive. On the weekend, head off to **Tulum★★**, **Cancún★★**, **Xcaret★★★**, or **Cobá★★**. With some of the basics down, make your way West to **Valladolid★★** (one day), spending the night here, or in **Chichén Itzá★★★** (one day) to tour the Mayan site early in the morning when it is quiet and the light is perfect for photos. Chichén Itzá is equally alluring in the fading evening light, before the sound and light show. You can spend another day enjoying the pampering of the Yaxkin Spa or adventuring at **Ik-Kil★★**. From here make your way west to **Mérida★★** to set up base camp in her colonial streets. After walking the town and doing some of your shopping (one day), you can set off on the **Ruta de los Conventos★** (one

Ruins of the observatory, Chichén Itzá

©Tom Dowd/Dreamstime.com

MUST KNOW

day), the **Ruta de las Haciendas**★ (one day), or the **Ruta Puuc**★ (one day). Finally, make the drive to the city of **Campeche**★ to enjoy the quiet of its fortressed cobblestone streets (one day), before flying to Cancún for your departure.

Tropical Birds

The Yucatán Peninsula is home to 546 bird species in 74 different families. They can be found almost everywhere, but particularly in and around Mayan ruins like **Chichén Itzá**★★★ and **Cobá**★★. For a three-day trip, start in **Mérida**★★. From here make your way to the town of **Dzemul**, to **Komchén de los Pájaros** (www.komchen.org). At this 340 hectare sanctuary of plants, animals, and people, you can spend an unusual vacation far from the madding crowd. Along with bird life, enjoy daily home-baked bread and ecologically friendly facilities. Take a jaunt by bike to **Xcambó**, **Telchac**, and the invisible Cretaceous crater in **Chicxulub**, left by a vast meteor, whose impact sent a vast cloud of debris into the sky that many believe led to the extinction of the dinosaurs. Or, drive along coastal

©Randy Plett/iStockphoto.com
Keel-billed toucan

Highway 27 to **Dzilam de Bravo** for a bird-watching tour by boat.

Colonial Cities

To visit the region's colonial gems follow conquistador Francisco de Montejo's route—backward— starting in **Valladolid**★★. Be sure to walk the Calle de los Frailes to the Convento de San Bernardino de Siena. From here, travel two hours to ochre **Izamal**★, where you can tour Bishop Landa's monumental San Antonio de Padua monastery built atop the ancient city's **Pop-hol-Chac** pyramid. Kinich the Sun God's even more monumental pyramid

©Innes Ferguson/BigStockPhoto.com
San Antonio de Padua monastery, Izamál

IDEAS AND TOURS

13

has a fantastic view of the city. From this spiritual center continue on to **Mérida★★**, and finally to **Campeche★**, from where you can buy a flight back to **Cancún★★**. With seven days to spare, you should have plenty of time.

The Convent Route

South from Mérida on Route18; stop at Acancéh, Tekoh, Telchaquillo, Tekit, Mama, Chumayel, Teabo and Maní (map; see Yucatán and West). The architecture of the 16C Franciscan monasteries of the Convent Route is unique among regional monasteries. You can visit the monasteries on a daytrip from **Mérida★★**, or over a couple of days from a local hacienda. These plain, austere buildings, with buttressed walls and few windows, are more like fortresses than churches, and were built not only for evangelization, but also to educate and urbanize the native population. The single most common external ornamentation in this zone is the bell gable, a decorative belfry. Smaller ones characterize the Guadalupe chapel in Acancéh, where a pyramid stands in the Town Square; others are ornamented like those in Tekit, scene

of bloody battles during the Caste War. Some bell gables are so large that they cover the whole facade, as is the case in Yotholín. Still others are connected by complicated pediments that resemble towers, like those in Ticul, or built in threes and ornately decorated, like those of Muna. The churches usually face west, with an attached monastery and open-air chapel, an orchard, a cemetery and a well. Most of the convents stand on the foundations of ancient Mayan temples and are enclosed by an atrium wall with corner chapels.

Yucatecán Cuisine

Begin your tour in **Mérida★★** with the Yucatán Express course at Los Dos Yucatecán Cooking School (*Calle 68 No. 517, Por 65 y 67 Colonia Centro, Mérida; 999-928-1116; www.los-dos.com*). The class will take a half-day (*9am–2pm*) and will introduce you to Yucatecán cuisine and its history, take you to the market, and leave the *sabor* of the Yucatán on your tongue. From here, day trips in all directions will delight your tourist palate. On your way to **Uxmal★★★**, stop in **Muna**'s central park to try grilled *poc chuc*. In **Izamal★**, enjoy a *sopa*

Windsurfing in Riviera Maya

©Svitlana Prada/iStockphoto.com

de lima and with *tanchucuá*, a local chocolate version of *atole*. In **Valladolid**★★ taste *pavo oriental*, the pride of the town. In **Progreso** try a new version of the same old fish fillet in *pescado tikin-xic*, baked in banana leaves. Taste each of these over three days of Yucatán exploration.

Southern Mayan Cities

With a week's vacation and a great sense of adventure, buy a one-way ticket to **Campeche**★ from **Cancún**★★. From here you can rent a car and set out to **Ednzá**★ and the many sites along the **Ruta Río Bec**★★. Highway 186 from Escárcega will take you through dense jungle where you can visit the sites of **Balamku**, **Becán**★★, **Chiccaná**★, **Calakmul**★★, **Xpuhil**★, **Kinichná**★, **Kohunlich**★★, and **Dzibanché**★. The route is wild and services are few and far between. In Xpuhil you will find several options for lodging, from bare to luxurious. Upon arrival at **Chetumal**★, if you have more time, you can continue up to **Cobá**★★ and beautiful **Tulum**★★, before sampling the beaches of the **Riviera Maya**★★★ on your return to Cancún.

Railway Tours

Take a week-long luxury train tour beginning in Villahermosa, Tabasco, and passing through Palenque, **Campeche**★, **Ednzá**★, **Mérida**★★, **Uxmal**★★★, **Izamal**★ and **Chichén Itzá**★★★. The Expreso Maya Train (*1-800-717-0108; www.expresomaya.com*) costs $2165–$4570 per person. Check the website for itineraries, prices and online booking.

IDEAS AND TOURS

CALENDAR OF EVENTS

Today the Yucatán counts its days by a modern calendar, but its events from joyous Fat Tuesday to the Day of the Dead are timeless.

JANUARY
New Year's Day
1 January.
Celebrations in all towns and cities. Look for *viejos*, stuffed dolls who may remain in the "flesh", but are more likely to have been turned to ashes at midnight.

Día de Los Reyes Magos
6 January.
Celebrations in all towns and cities. Translated as Day of the Three Kings, at this festival you break a *rosca de reyes* to see who needs to make the tamales for February 2.

FEBRUARY
Día de la Candelaria
2 February.
Celebrations where the Candelaria is the patroness, such as Candelaria, Campeche.

Mayakoba Golf Classic
First two weeks of February.
Riviera Maya, Cancún.
www.mayakobagolfclassic.com.

Carnaval
Late January to late February.
Throughout Latin America the tradition of Carnaval around **Fat Tuesday** is a delight to the sensations. Parades feature dance groups in bright costumes, whimsically decorated floats, and individuals in amazingly fanciful costumes. Children and adults join in, with music and dancing, fairs, food and plenty of fun for all.

Campeche
www.carnavaldecampeche.com.
Cancún
www.carnavalcancun.com.
Cozumel
www.thisiscozumel.com.
Mérida
www.merida.gob.mx/carnaval.

MARCH
Día de Benito Juarez
21 March. National Holiday.
This day commemorates the birth of Mexico's only indigenous president, native to Oaxaca state.

Spring Equinox
21 March, **Chichén Itzá**.
The ancient cosmological genius of the Mayans is relived each Equinox as the Feathered Serpent Kukulcán descends the steps of his temple in a play of light drawn by the sun.

February: Carnaval in Cozumel

© Cozumel Promotion Board

APRIL
Semana Santa
Late March or Early April.
Holy Week. Celebrations in all towns and cities. Do not be alarmed if you come across men being crucified in a live representation of Christ's dramatic death.

Feria de la Miel
13–17 April.
Hopelchén, Campeche.
In a land where honey has always reigned, it is duly celebrated each year at the Honey Fair with popular and folkloric dances, fireworks, music, parades, and competitions.

MAY
Día del Trabajo
1 May.
National Holiday, Labor Day. Celebrations in all towns and cities.

Día de la Cruz
3 May.
Formerly an official Catholic day, this day still celebrates builders and construction workers.

El Cedral Festival
25 April–5 May, **Cozumel**.
The El Cedral Festival was started about 150 years ago by Casimiro Cardenas who escaped to Cozumel clutching a wooden cross after his village was attacked in the War of the Castes. The festival honors the power of the cross. Fairs, traditional feasts, rodeos, music, competitions and the crowning of the queen.

5 de Mayo
5 May. National Holiday.
This day commemorates the Battle of Puebla; you will definitely find other *extranjeros* drinking plenty of Corona at local bars.

Día de la Madres
10 May.
National Holiday. Celebrations of mothers in all towns and cities, with parades, dinners or dances.

Celebrations of Patron Saint
19 and 20 May.
Xcambo (Xtampu) Ruins, Yucatán. If you would like to visit these small ruins near the coast of Yucatán, think about going on these days to take part in local festivities which are sure to include dancing, food and drink.

Cozumel Boat Rodeo and Fishing Tournament
Last two weeks of May.
Isla Cozumel. More than 100 boats participate each year in this sport fishing event.

La Travesia Sigrada Maya
End of May, **Cozumel**, **Xcaret**.
The Mayan Sacred Journey.
www.travesiasagradamaya.com.mx
An annual reenactment of one of the most important traditions of the Mayan people—the pilgrimage to Cozumel to pay tribute to the Goddess Ix Chel.

JUNE
Día de La Marina, Seaman's day
1 June, **Progreso**.
General festivities occur throughout this port town on this day. The weekend that falls closest is host to a sailboat regatta.

Festival of San Pedro and San Pablo
29 June, **Cozumel**.
The celebration of these two saints usually coincides with the begin-

ning of the rainy season. This day is remembered annually in Cozumel with dances, parades, local gastronomy and fun for all.

AUGUST
Fiesta de la Virgen de la Asunción
15 August, Muna, Yucatán.
The patroness of the plain but elegant Cathedral of Muna is celebrated with music and stalls.

SEPTEMBER
Ironman 70.3 Cancún
September,
Playa Langosta, Cancún.
www.triathlon.org.
The world triathlon community turns its eyes to Cancún each year to see who will be the next champion of air, wind and water. In November there is another Ironman event in Cozumel.

Día de la Independencia
15 and 16 September.
Celebrations in all towns and cities; check Isla Mujeres and Cozumel, or any central square nearing midnight on the 15th for the "Grito".

Autumn Equinox
21 September, Chichén Itzá.
For those traveling in the fall, this date and those surrounding it provide the chance to witness the phenomenon of Quetzalcoatl's return to the Earth from the Astros.

Día de San Miguel Arcangel
29 September, Cozumel.
Parades across the island inaugurate the festivities in honor of Saint Michael, Patron Saint of this idyllic island.

OCTOBER
Día de la Raza
12 October, National Holiday.
Declared "Day of the Races" in 1992 by national governments throughout the Americas. What was once called Columbus Day now remembers the indigenous peoples that his fleets encountered upon arrival, and their descendents.

Pilgrimage to Izamal, Cristo Negro
18 October, Izamal.
Pilgrims from all over Mexico come to pay homage in the procession of the Black Christ.

Riviera Maya Underground Film Festival
Mid-October, Playa del Carmen.
www.rmuff.com.
Underground films from all over the World are shown in various venues throughout town.

NOVEMBER
Día de los Muertos
1 and 2 November.
Celebrations in all towns and cities of All Saint's Day, thought to be the days when the departed return to enjoy the worldly treasures they sought in life.

The **Day of the Dead** is an ancient festival that sees Mexican families remember and pay homage to their dead, as well as celebrating the continuation of life, embodied by children. Usually a two-day festival, the first day celebrates loved ones who have passed on, and the second celebrates children. Sugar skeletons and other items with death motifs are given to friends and family. Families plan picnics with all the foods their loved ones liked, and decorate towns and villages so that the departed are tempted back, as well as baking *Pan de Muerto*. This "bread of the dead" is prepared by many families and chefs all over Mexico for this very special celebration. In the area of Oaxaca, you will find it shaped into a body or burial wrap with a face embedded on the end of the loaf. Because of the demand for the "bread of the dead" during this time many bakeries halt production of other breads.

Yucatán Bird Festival "TOH"
First two weeks of November, Mérida.
www.yucatanbirds.org.mx.
The birds of the Yucatán are celebrated in their own festival, which consists of lectures, activities, and competitions.

Día de la Revolución
19 and 20 November.
National Holiday. Celebrations in all towns and cities; see Cancún and Cozumel.

Mayan Riviera Gay Fall Festival
Mid-November, Cancún.
www.gaymexicoexperts.com.
Downtown Cancún is painted with all the colors of the rainbow each year when its bars and clubs help the gay community to delight in celebration for celebration's sake. Arco Iris, Mexico's leading gay tour guide, also organizes special tours and cruises.

Riviera Maya Jazz Festival
Late November, Mamitas Beach, Playa del Carmen.
www.rivieramayajazzfestival.com.
Local and International jazz artists play in several venues (free entry).

DECEMBER
Fiesta de la Virgen de Izamal
8 December.
Pilgrims from all over Mexico come to honor the miraculous healing power of the Virgin in the Convento de San Antonio de Padua in Izamal.

Fiesta de la Virgen de Guadalupe
11 and 12 December.
Patroness of Mérida and Mexico. Celebrations in all towns and cities.

Las Posadas
16–24 December.
Celebrations in all towns, commemorating Mary and Joseph's journey and search for an inn.

Noche Buena
24 December.
Christmas Eve is always an occasion for celebration.

Navidad
25 December.
Christmas Day is a national holiday. All towns and cities join the celebrations.

Día de los Inocentes
28 December.
The "day of the innocents" is Mexico's April Fool's Day, so be wary who you believe on this day.

PRACTICAL INFORMATION

MUST KNOW

WHEN TO GO

High season in the Yucatán officially spans mid-Dec to mid-Apr, and always includes Holy Week; the eight days that lead up to Easter. Low season has traditionally been May–Dec 15th, when prices drop 10–30%. Some hotels and services are beginning to charge high-season rates in the summer months when schools are on holiday, though they may still charge less than they do in the winter. The weather is hot and humid year-round, though May is perhaps the most consistent hottest month. Hurricane season, officially from June to November, can hit the region hard, as it has in recent years. If you would like to see flamingos in droves in **Celestún★★**, be sure to go between November and May. If you would like to see them in **Ría Lagartos**, go between May and November. You can swim with whale sharks by **Isla Holbox★★** from Jul–mid-Sept and by **Isla Contoy★★** Apr–Oct.

KNOW BEFORE YOU GO

Books

Pedro Paramo, *Juan Rulfo. (1955; 1994).* Gabriel Garcia Marquez called this "the most beautiful of all stories that have been written in the Spanish language." This novel, first published in Mexico in 1955, is a literary masterpiece that captures the cadence and the heartbreak of Mexico.
Incidents of Travel in the Yucatán, *John Lloyd Stephens & Frederick Catherwood.* This classic text is an essential for the pocket of the informed traveler. First published in 1843, it features written accounts and marvelous drawings from the first English speakers to explore the Mayan region and write of their experiences.
The Mexico Reader: History, Culture, Politics, *Gilbert M. Joseph, ed. (2002).* Exploring Mexico's rich history and culture.
Popol Vuh, *Dennis Tedlock.* Translation of one of the most important texts in the native languages of the Americas. Called "the Mayan Bible" by many academics, it recounts the Mayan people's origins.
The Code of Kings, *Linda Schele and Peter Mathews.* This book studies seven of the most famous buildings in Mayan archeology, illustrating how the Maya used glyphs to inscribe their architecture with history and mythology.
Michelin Green Guide Mexico. A regional guide to the very best that Mexico has to offer.

Useful Websites

www.visitmexico.com – National portal for Mexico's tourism board.
www.mayayucatan.com.mx/en– The government's in depth Yucatán tourism website.
www.islacozumel.com.mx – CozumelTourism Board.
www.campechetravel.com – Campeche Tourism Boars.
www.travelyucatan.com – Tourist information and online reservations.
www.yucatantoday.com – A wonderfully informative magazine that provides history and insider tips. Pick up a printed copy

in hotels, restaurants and retail stores around the Yucatán.

www.locogringo.com – The place for a local gringo's advice on Cancún and the Riviera Maya.

www.mayanroutes.com – Information on a comprehensive list of pre-Hispanic sites.

www.mostlymaya.com – Useful practical information along with history and reflection for many sites off the beaten path, such as those along the Ruta Río Bec.

www.yucatanwildlife.com – Online guide to wildlife watching and eco-tourism in the Yucatán.

www.yucatanliving.org – Provides anecdotal information and an inside look into life in and around Mérida, from the point of view of American expatriates. The website gives a good idea of what the growing expat community is up to, including weekly events in the area, and local charities.

Tourism Offices

Cancún – Blvd. Kukulcan Km 9 Cancun Center 1er. Piso, Zona Hotelera, Cancún. 998-881-2745 http://cancun.travel/en

Campeche – Secretaría de Turismo del Estado: Plaza Moch Couoh, Centro, 981-816-6767, www.campeche.travel

Mérida – Modulo de Información Turística: Calle 60 between 57 & 59, Centro, 924-0000, www.merida.gob.mx/turisimo

Yucatán – Secretaria de Turismo, 999-930-3760, www.mayayucatan.com.mx/en

International Visitors

Embassies

Australia – Ruben Dario 55, Col. Polanco, Mexico DF. 1101 2200.

Canada – Schiller 529, Col. Polanco, Mexico DF. 5274-7900.

United Kingdom – Río Lerma 71, Mexico DF. 5242-8500.

United States – Paseo de la Reforma 305, Mexico DF. 5080-2000.

Entry Requirements

All visitors who plan to stay for more than 72 hours need a Mexican **tourist card** or **FMT** (*Folleto de Migración Turística*). If you fly to Mexico you will be given one before you disembark and pass through customs. They are available from government tourist offices, travel agents, and border offices at points of entry. Business travelers must ask for a Business Entry Form (*Formulato Migratorio de Negocios*).

Foreign visitors entering Mexico must carry proof of citizenship, preferably a valid passport and, in some cases, a **visa**. Citizens of the United States, Canada, the United Kingdom, Ireland, Australia, New Zealand and some Western European countries do not need visas to enter Mexico as tourists. The maximum stay as a tourist is 180 days.

Children under 18 years of age who are traveling alone or with a guardian need an authorized statement from their parents, unless the minor has a valid passport.

Tourist cards must be returned to Mexican immigration officials at the time of departure. If you do not have one you can expect hassles, delays, and a fine of $40 minimum.

Make a photocopy of both your FMT (*see above*) and passport's photo page, and pack them separately from the actual documents.

Customs Regulations

Mexican law allows you to enter with two one-liter bottles of alcoholic beverages; 400 cigarettes (2 cartons) or 20 cigars (if the person carrying them is over 18 years of age); and gifts that do not exceed $300.

Illegal drugs, plants and perishable goods, firearms and weapons of any kind are all forbidden. Check with the Mexican embassy or consulate before entering the country if you have any questions regarding the strict regulations on importing firearms for hunting. The export of archeological objects is forbidden.

Health

Before You Go – Prior to departure, check with your insurance company for their policies concerning emergency consultations, medical expenses, medication and hospitalization while abroad. All prescription drugs should be properly labeled and accompanied by a copy of the prescription. Bring more than enough of all prescription medications from home, and carry them in your hand luggage. Mexican equivalents of US prescription medications are rather expensive and brand names are different to those in the US. Remember to bring sun screen.

Bites and Stings – Mosquitoes are found along the coast and in the Yucatán lowlands: bring strong insect repellent. Most visitors will never see a scorpion, but if you are stung, see a doctor immediately (toxin antidote is readily available in Mexico's pharmacies).

Disease – There is risk of **malaria** in the states of Campeche, Chiapas, Guerrero, Michoacán, Nayarit, Oaxaca, Quintana Roo, Sinaloa and Tabasco. **Dengue Fever** is on the increase all over the world and there have been a few outbreaks in the Mayan region. Avoid swimming in stagnant water, use insect repellent, cover up and sleep under netting. For additional information, US residents can contact the Centers for Disease Control and Prevention (CDC), Atlanta GA; (404) 332-4559 or www.cdc.gov.

Sanitation – Drinking bottled water is recommended. In most tourist areas, fresh salads are now treated before preparation, and ice is OK for drinking; elsewhere they are best avoided.

Pharmacies – Pharmacies are easy to find in all towns and cities. Throughout Mexico pharmacies provide medical assistance for minor illness. An effective medicine for gastrointestinal problems is Lomotil, available at pharmacies.

Doctors – Red Cross clinics accept walk-ins, while doctor consultations in private practices generally charge a $30 consultation fee.

Hospitals – In case of medical emergency, check at the hotel's front desk for a listing of English speaking doctors and hospitals with English speaking staff. There are hospitals and clinics in most major towns along the coast and in regional centers like Mérida (in an emergency, dial 060).

Accessibility

Disabled Travelers – Unfortunately sidewalks are an afterthought at best on the narrow cobblestone streets of most colonial centers. This can make getting around in a wheelchair quite a challenge. Fortunately, in Mexico it should not be hard to

come across people who are willing to help should it be necessary. Cancún, built more recently, is a bit more wheelchair friendly. Disabled people are not charged admission to any of the peninsula's archeological sites. **Chichén Itzá★★★** is particularly easy to get around, as is **Xcaret★★★**. In **Cancún★★**, the Camino Real Cancún (Paseo Kukulcán, km 9.5, Punta Cancún; 998 8830100 www.camino-real.com) is recommended for its "handicapped room", while in **Valladolid★★** you can find a suite especially designed for wheel chair access at the guest house and spa Casa Hamaca (Parque San Juan, Calle 49 N° 202-A x 40; 985-856-5287; www.casahamaca.com).
Senior Citizens – Climbing pyramids is not for the faint of heart and it is best to make slow and steady progress if you are feeling up to it. The young at heart should not miss dancing on Saturday night in Mérida's Plaza Mayor, where you will be accompanied by youngsters upward of 70 dancing to the rhythms of *danzones,* popular music from yesteryear.

GETTING THERE AND AROUND

By Air
Cancún International Airport (998-848-7200; 998-886-0322; www.cancun-airport.com) is serviced by major international airlines with non-stop flights from major US and some European cities. There is a shuttle between Cancún and Cozumel that makes several round trips a day. Domestic and some US airlines run services to **Cozumel Airport** and **Mérida International Airport** (connect-ing flights to **Cozumel** and **Chetumal**). The airports at Mérida and **Campeche** are most serviced by flights from Mexico City's **Benito Juárez International Airport**. Taxi service and car rental agencies are available at all airports.

By Ship
International **cruise ships** dock at Progreso, Cozumel, Playa del Carmen and Mahahual. *For more information, see 'Sailing and Cruising' chapters in the MUST SEE section.*

By Coach/Bus
Bus terminals in the main cities provide transportation to tourist sights throughout the region.
ADO and luxury buses – www.ticketbus.com.mx, 1-800-702-8000.
ADO Cancún Airport – 998-886-0871.

By Car
The Yucatán is a driver's delight: main roads throughout the peninsula are paved and in good condition, though minor roads may require a four-wheel drive. Driving here is safe but travelers are advised to make sure their vehicle is in good working condition, and to keep the tank topped up as roads outside major towns and tourist areas may stretch endless distances between gas stations. Avoid driving at night and use toll roads wherever possible.
Car rental – If you plan to hire a car, you should reserve one in advance online or over the phone. For online reservations try www.kimbila.com (Mérida), or www.cancunrentacar.com (Cancún Airport, downtown, and Riviera Maya).

Car Rental Companies
Avis 1-800-288-8888.
www.avis.com
Budget (55) 5705-5061.
www.budget.com
Hertz 1-800-709-5000.
www.hertz.com
Europcar 1-800-201-2084.
www.europcar.com
Alamo 1-800-849-8001 /
1101-1100.
www.alamo-mexico.com.mx

Car rental agencies are located in all major cities and airports. For further advice on car rental and driving in the area, try www.travelyucatan.com.

Rules of the Road – On all public roads, drive on the right-hand side. Cars may overtake each other on the left, and often do so quite freely. The speed limit is indicated in kilometers/hour. In cities, the speed limit is 50km/hr (30mph). On highways it is 100km/hr (60mph) during the day and 90km/hr (55mph) at night. At night be wary of cars that might not have working head and tail lights. Be careful at railroad crossings. Seatbelts are mandatory.

Highways – A six-lane *cuota* highway (toll road) connects Mérida with Cancún within four hours. Route 307 runs four lanes from Cancún to Tulum; these are often congested with heavy traffic.

Breakdown – The Angeles Verdes provide bi-lingual roadside service on highways (dial 078).

Gasoline – Available in any PEMEX station: Magna Sin (unleaded, green pumps), Premium (performance unleaded, red pumps). Most stations are open 6am–10pm. There is no self-service and it is customary to tip the attendant ($.2–$.5).

Speed bumps – Be wary of home made *topes*, or speed bumps, which you are likely to find each time the highway passes through a populated area. They can often be steep as a pyramid, so you really should proceed with caution.

Parking – There are no meters here, nor are there seas of parking lots surrounding places you want to get to. At archeological sites you will find lots, some of which charge, while others do not. In cities, street parking is often the most convenient option. Yellow and red curbs denote no-parking areas. Double parking is illegal, though it can be quite common practice. In Mérida watch for men on red tricycles or waving red flags. These are self-appointed street parking attendants, and may well provide you with a very useful service. You must pay them whatever amount of pesos you deem appropriate in exchange for their help. In many lots attendants will direct you into sometimes tight spots. Tipping is also expected here.

Public Transportation

City Buses – All cities have bus circuits that are generally cheap, clean and reliable. Inquire at local tourist offices for city-specific routes and schedules.

Taxis – Taxis are a convenient and relatively economical way to get around. In most urban as well as rural areas, some sort of taxi, combi, or pickup service is most likely available. Thankfully, taxi in Spanish is pronounced almost the same as in English. Do not be afraid to ask those in the know for advice when you find yourself at an impasse.

BASIC INFORMATION

Accommodations

For a list of suggested accommodations, see Must Stay.

Hotel Reservation Services – For accommodations in the Riviera Maya be sure to check with the Loco Gringo (www.locogringo. com) for comparative information on available lodging, and to make reservations. Wanderplanet (www. wanderplanet.com) has some discount bookings, as does www.mayan-world.com.

Hostels – Look for hostels online at www.hostelworld.com, which provides information and booking for hostels in many areas.

Business Hours

Banks are usually open Mon–Fri 9am–1:30pm and in larger cities on Saturday 9am–noon. Businesses and retail stores tend to operate Mon–Sat 9am–8pm. Government offices, including tourist offices, are open Mon–Fri 8:30am–7pm. These schedules, of course, vary from town to town. In many if not most places, businesses close at the hour of the *comida*, or mid-day meal, from noon–2pm.

On national holidays and sometimes during the celebrations of patron saints, banks, government offices, schools and some businesses are closed.

Communications

Telephones – Phone calls can be made from Ladatel pay phones, for which you can find a prepaid Ladatel card at almost any store or pharmacy, or in call booths that advertise their service with signs that read *"se hacen llamadas telefónicas"*, or similar.

Area Codes – *Campeche*: 981 (in the city), 982, 996, and 997. *Quintana Roo*: 983, 984, 997, 998 (Cancún and Isla Mujeres), and 987 (Cozumel). *Yucatán*: 985, 986, 988, 991 and 999 (Mérida).

Internet – The Internet is widely available throughout Mexico and especially in tourist areas. Prices at internet cafés, many of which now have wireless connections, should be around 10 pesos per hour.

Mail – Mail in most areas of Mexico is rapidly becoming dependable. Post offices are open Mon–Fri from 8am–5pm, and some on Saturday mornings. Airmail to Europe takes about 6 days. Sometimes ground mail within Mexico and to foreign addresses can be slow.

Postage for international letters weighing 20g is $3. You may also receive mail at the post office by registering poste restante.

For more information, contact the post office, in Mérida at Calle 53 between 53 and 54; in Campeche in the Palacio Federal on Av. 16 de Septiembre; or in Cancún downtown near the Mercado 28, at Sunyaxchen and Tankah.

You can also call the Central Post Office in Mexico City, 5709-9600 or 5222-9500, for further information.

Special Delivery – Independent carriers, such as DHL and FedEx, provide overnight mail and post to and from major cities.

DHL, **Mérida**:

Calle 22 # 323 Entre 13 y 13A, Col. Ampl. Ciudad Industrial, Mérida, 97288; 999-946-1421, 999-946-1432, 999-946-1434.

FedEx, **Mérida**:

Av. Internacional #809, at Calle 108, Col. Nueva Sámbula, Mérida,

Yucatán, 97250. Open Mon–Fri 9am–6pm.

Discounts

Senior Citizens – Most museums and all archeological sites have seniors discounts with a valid I.D. In Mexico, the term to describe seniors is 'tercer edad'.

Students – Student discounts are available with a valid I.D. at many sites of interest.

Electricity

Voltage is 120 volts AC, 60Hz. Adapters and flat plugs are available at local electric stores, or bring your own from home.

Media

Yucatán Today can be found in print in tourist offices and hotels in Mérida. www.yucatantoday.com.

Diario de Yucatán is the state's daily paper. www.yucatan.com.mx.

Novedades Quintana Roo is a daily Spanish-language paper that covers Cancún, Isla Mujeres, Cozumel and Playa del Carmen.

Cancún Tips is an English language magazine that you may well be given at Cancún airport. www.cancuntips.com.mx.

Magazine Xcaret gives unique information on the area in English. www.xcaretmagazine.com.

Money

In this guide, prices are quoted in US dollars, using an exchange rate of approx 10 Mexican pesos to $1 USD.

Mexico's major banks are **Banamex** and **Bancomer**. Mexican currency is the peso, available in coins and paper bills. Local businesses often charge in US dollars as well as pesos. Remember that current exchange rates apply when you pay for a dollar-quoted tour in Mexican pesos. Changing dollars is not difficult, but you should be armed with plenty of pesos when traveling to lesser known haunts. Likewise, do not count on finding an ATM outside of major cities. Getting change can be difficult, so try to break notes in larger stores and carry a lot of small bills and change. Do not accept damaged bills as banks won't accept them.

Restaurants

For a list of suggested restaurants, see *Must Eat*. For discount bookings, try: www.cancun-discounts.com, www.cancunandrivieramaya.com.

Safety

Personal – For emergencies contact the National Center for Communication and Civil Protection (**CENACOM**), 1-800-004-13. Persons needing legal assistance should contact Protección Legal al Turista (**SECTUR**) at 250-6603 (English). Local police forces, especially in Mexico City, are often slow in handling emergencies (robbery, car jacking, etc.); foreigners may be better served by contacting the hotel management, the tourism office or the embassy or consulate.

Beaches/Sea – Respect signs that limit swimming or boating as well as buoys that divide the area designated for swimming from the open sea. Occasionally there are red flags that indicate an

Measurement Equivalents									
Degrees Fahrenheit	95°	86°	77°	68°	59°	50°	41°	32°	23°	14°
Degrees Celsius	35°	30°	25°	20°	15°	10°	5°	0°	-5°	-10°

1 inch = 2.5 centimeters	1 foot = 30.5 centimeters
1 mile = 1.6 kilometers	1 pound = 0.4 kilograms
1 quart = 0.9 liters	1 gallon = 3.8 liters

extremely dangerous, forbidden area. Supervise children at all times. In the event of an accident, immediately advise a lifeguard or hotel authorities. Some beaches have jellyfish that sting. Be aware of sea urchins, while further out at sea you should watch for moray eels and sharks. When diving, make sure you are accompanied by someone who knows the area.

Smoking

While smoking is still widely accepted in almost all public places in Mexico, lawmakers are working on putting a stop to it. Cigarettes are widely available, but if you are in a hotel or restaurant or other public space, it is advisable to enquire before lighting up. The new law proposes up to 36 hours in **jail** for illicit smoking.

Spectator Sports

Baseball is a national sport in Mexico, and games here are sure to be an unforgettable experience for fans accustomed to American comportment in the bleachers. In Mérida you can check for a game with the Leones de Yucatán between the end of March and the end of August, at their website www.leonesdeyucatan.com.mx. Also look for the Tigres de Cancún, and the Piratas de Campeche at www.piratasdecampeche.com.mx.

Tax

A Federal Tax called the **IVA** is now charged on food and medicine, as well as many other articles. There are plans to launch a tax refund system at major airports in 2009.

Time

The Yucatán peninsula lies within the **Central Time Zone**. Government, businesses, schools, and transport services throughout Mexico move their clocks forward one hour beginning the first Sunday in April, and back again the last Sunday in October. It is common, however, to come across clocks and sometimes even entire towns that do not reflect this change. People may refer to "God's time" (*tiempo de Dios*) and "Calderón's time" (the current President). "Mexican Time" is a phenomenon in its own right, and has a reputation for testing patience.

Tipping

In general, a 15% tip is appreciated by any worker in the service industry. Give tips to gas station attendants, windshield washers and those that help you park your car.

Bribery is no longer what it once was in Mexico and offering bribes will land you in trouble. Be careful and very polite if asked for one by an official.

CANCÚN AND YUCATÁN

Mayab—land of the Maya, land of prophecy and patience. Humankind has walked this porous limestone peninsula since 3000BC. First hunter-gatherers, then agriculturalists with complex irrigation systems, then lords of great cities and masters of the arts and sciences—the Mayan people have stepped before you in every cave, cenote, village and city that you visit. Though you will see the vestiges of cities abandoned some hundreds of years past, the Maya are still present, and their prophetic legacy still points toward a fast-approaching future.

In villages across Mayan Meso-America—from the jeweled waters of the Yucatán to the cloud draped mountains of Guatemala and Chiapas—a day-keeper keeps count of the days. Long before our historians began writing their books, the Maya began to remember a sacred cycle, called **The Long Count**, which comes to a close in 2012. The calendar is based upon ancient events in these very skies, observed at the height of the Classic Mayan renaissance from the Caracol-like towers you will visit in **Chichén Itzá★★★** and **Mayapán★**.

Not a single river runs atop this limestone plank that stretches north, from the dense jungle of today's border with Guatemala, toward the emerald and turquoise waters of its Gulf and Caribbean shores. Fresh water comes from rain and subterranean oases that dot the peninsula in some 3,000 cenotes, of which only half are known by written registry. In the ancient cities one face above all others will meet you; that of **Chaac, God of Rain**. His elephantine nose is associated with the bolts of lighting that often accompany the arrival of his important blessings: his power so vital to the people of the Yucatán that he is honored in a mesmerizing litany of forms—in the rows of masks that line palaces and temples like that at **Kabah★**.

For millennia the Maya have lived here, planting their *milpas* in what

Mayan warrior depicted in relief, Chichén Itzá

soil can be salvaged from among the stone, building their epic cities or their modern fences with the stones they lift in the sowing of seeds. They have also maintained an unending cycle of rituals that sustain this fragile Eden, where the same jaguars for which their ancient temples are named still roam freely.

The drought that marked the end of the **Classical Period** throughout Mexico in the year **AD900** was also a change in the tides for the Mayan region. It is thought to have driven the Itzá from today's **Campeche★** to **Chichén★★★**—regional capital of the Maya—in **AD980**. At the same time, Toltecs from the city of Tula in central Mexico arrived following an expelled priest-king named for the god **Quetzalcoatl**, the feathered serpent, who is called **Kukulcán** by the Maya. The militarized hierarchy that accompanied him stayed in power following Kukulcán's disappearance into the grass of the ball court, which symbolizes the universe, and is the playing field for a game that represents the struggle between light and darkness. Here the feathered serpent made a promise that he would return to end this world in order to bring it back to the light. The region broke into warring city-states, most of which were ruined by the **15th century**. Kukulcán's Castillo at Chichén Itzá "city on the edge of the water-sorcerer's well," was long abandoned when the **Spanish** arrived at the shores of Campeche in 1517. Though the warriors who met them kept the Spanish at bay for a while, by 1540 the pyramids were being dismantled by conquistadors and the Catholic Church in order to build their homes and monasteries atop the crumbled foundations. They rode in on the very **sacbés**—"white roads"—made by the Maya to link cities throughout the peninsula.

By the **19th century** the descendents of full-blooded Spaniards, mixed mestizos, and the Maya were living side by side – but separate—in a strictly vertical society wherein the Maya were the slave labor of the landowning elite. The manufacture of agave into sturdy sisal fiber, used to tie up the sails on the boats that were stripping the jungle of precious woods, turned the owners of haciendas into the elite. With revenues from their precious "green gold", and influenced as much by Cuba, Europe and the US as by the Mexican mainland, the ruling class began to push toward secession in the glorious days of the first half of the century. Their grandeur halted when the Mayan people were given arms by British Honduras, and took back their lands, though briefly. The Yucatán's brutal **Caste Wars** voiced the first call of what became the Mexican Revolution of 1910.

It was not until the **1960s**, when modern road and rail linked the peninsula to the national network, that the Yucatán was brought into the folds of the nation. In the 1970s **Cancún★★** received its first influx of investment and its conversion into the world's defining super destination began. Today, tourism development throughout the region has lead to a new invasion of sorts—explorers who come from afar to experience and share in this most unique of places, with this most dignified of peoples.

CANCÚN★★

Cancún★★ and the nearby islands of **Mujeres★★** and **Contoy★★** have one great asset: the sea. This natural marine playground, sparkling under the warm sun, is caressed by breezes that keep the temperature a comfortable average 25°C/80°F. Mile after mile of Caribbean beaches and the 29sq km/18sq mi of the **Nichupté Lagoon★** make Cancún a watersports and beach holiday mecca. Active visitors can do everything from 🤿 **scuba diving** and 🤿 **snorkeling** to parasailing, before exploring the remains of local **Mayan settlements** and the natural kingdoms hiding in the area's **cenotes** (*see Cozumel and South*), **bird colonies** and **coastal reefs**. Pristine nature reserves are in easy reach with a short boat trip to Isla Contoy or Isla Mujeres, as well as excursions to stunning natural sites like **Xcaret★★★** and **Xel-Há★★** (*see Cozumel and South*). Cancún is the perfect base for day trips to Mayan archeological ruins like **Tulum★★** and **Cobá★★** (*see Cozumel and South*), as well as to Yucatán heartland sites like **Chichén Itzá★★★** (*see Yucatán and West*). **Children** are particularly well cared for here, with major resort hotels providing family services, while the region itself is a discovery land of adventure (*see Kids*).

CITY

Cancún, the consummate beach resort, first started development in 1970 after it was supposedly plucked from thin air by a computer tasked with finding the perfect location for a new resort. Since then it has re-invented itself several times over. On the east coast of the Yucatán Peninsula, Cancún is divided into two parts: on the mainland is **El Centro** (Downtown), home to Cancún's tourism workers. Isla Cancún contains the **Zona Hotelera★★** (Hotel Zone). It is connected to the mainland at both ends and bordered on the north by the **Bahía de Mujeres**, (**beaches★★★**) on the east by Caribbean Sea (**beaches★★**), and on the west and south by the **Nichupté Lagoon★**.

Getting There & Around

Most North American international carriers operate routes to Cancún,

Aerial View, Cancún

while a number of regional airlines (such as AeroMexico, Mexicana and Click Mexicana) provide local and international services. Car rental firms are well represented at the airport (*for companies and contact details see Planning Your Trip*).

The Zona Hotelera is a 10km/ 6mi/20min drive from the airport, with taxis costing around $25 to El Centro and $28–$40 to the Zona Hotelera. *Collectivos* (vans) are cheaper ($10), but aren't an option going back to the airport. Tickets are available at the airport terminal. Take Highway 180 east if coming by car from **Mérida★★** (80km/50mi away) or **Campeche★** (*see Yucatán and West*). If arriving by bus ($4 from airport), the ADO bus terminal is in El Centro at the intersection of avenidas Tulum and Uxmal, with connecting services throughout Mexico. Once you have arrived, rental cars, mopeds, bicycles, taxis, or buses (regular services; lots of stops; 6.5 pesos) make it easy get around.

El Centro

Here you can shop and eat with the locals for less. Tourists rarely *need* to go downtown, but it is a must for those who want a taste of real-life Mexico, rather than the enclosed beach world of the hotel zone. Streets are named after Mayan cities; **Avenida Tulum** at the center is home to the bus station and plenty of shopping. Nearby **Avenida Yaxchilán** is good for restaurants and nightlife, while **Mercado 28** is the town's main market.

CANCÚN COAST

Punta Arenas
Isla Contoy ★★
Isla Contoy Bird Sanctuary ★★
Isla Blanca
Laguna Chakmochuk
Isla Mujeres ★★
Punta Sam
El Meco
★★Cancún Puerto Juárez
Punta Cancún ★★
Hidalgo 180
Laguna de Nichupté ★
Wet n' Wild
0   10 km
307 Punta Tahchacté

Zona Hotelera★★

The hotel zone is a 12km/7mi-long series of hotels and condos, (sometimes so close together that you can't see the water) built along glorious **beach★★★** on the Caribbean Sea, backed by the **Nichupté Lagoon★**.
Canal Sigfrido at the north end of the island, right after the Nichupté Bridge, is a nice quiet spot to stop and watch the world go by. The next stop is **Punta Cancún★★**, the hub of the island's activity, set in the northeast corner and overshadowed by vast Vegas-style mega resorts. Punta Cancún is also home to the island's big nightclubs (*see Nightlife*) and many bars and restaurants. Everything in Punta Cancún is within walking distance, but heading south from there you should take a taxi or bus. South from Punta Cancún, the massive four-lane **Boulevard Kukulcán** runs the length of the island. Points along Blvd. Kukulcán are measured by kilometer markers. Shops, restaurants and services abound along this main artery,

usually immediately opposite the hotels. The boulevard is an endless shopper's paradise, its heart found at **Km12**'s massive malls like the **Flamingo Plaza** and **La Isla** (*see Shopping*). You can find some excellent bargains in Kukulcán's myriad shops (especially jewelry), but you may have to explore at length as prices in general are higher here than many other places in Mexico.

Further south lie some of Cancún's most popular beaches, such as **Playa Delfines** (*see Beaches*), as well as Cancún's Mayan ruins in residence, **El Rey**.

Daytrips

If you don't fancy heading down the coast (*see Cozumel & South*), or out into the Yucatán (*see Yucatán and West*), most visitors spend at least a day exploring **Isla Mujeres★★** or **Isla Contoy★★**. In addition to ferry services (*see Isla Mujeres below*), plenty of inclusive daytrip pleasure boat operators ply their trade from Cancún's **Playa Linda pier** (*see Sailing and Cruising*).

Isla Mujeres Coast
©Pictures Colour Library

For an alternative to the Mujeres ferry, try a skippered yacht tour such as **La Pinta** (*www.kolumbustours.com, 998-884-5333*), a replica of Christopher Columbus's ship, which departs to Isla Mujeres and Isla Contoy (*see Sailing and Cruising*). Various boats provide **scuba diving** and **snorkeling**; book at your nearest dive shop, or from hotel tour desks (*see Meso-American Reef*).

ISLA MUJERES★★

Isla Mujeres, just 6km/4mi off the coast, was likely the first point the Spanish set foot on when they came to Mexico. Some say that the huge number of female-shaped figurines they found there (offerings to Ixchel, goddess of fertility) led them to name it the 'Island of Women' (*Isla Mujeres*).

The Spanish moved on and left the island unoccupied, until 350 years later settlers from the Yucatán and Caribbean started to move here, building the brightly colored Caribbean houses that are still a vibrant characteristic of the island. The island is only 7.5km/5mi long and .7km/.5mi wide with a four- by six-block downtown. At the north end, the sandy streets of **Isla Town★** are the first thing that greet you when you disembark from the ferry. The diminutive settlement has small town appeal, but head out of town on the main road (Av. Rueda Medina) and you will pass **Hacienda Mundaca**, an ex-slaver's house, the inlet of **Laguna Macax** (a safe haven for boats, **swimming with dolphins**, a turtle sanctuary and good snorkeling), and ultimately arrive at the once spectacular snorkeling available at **Garrafón**

Natural Reef Park, part of **Faro Celerain**, the island's most southerly tip. Scuba aficionados need not stop here, as Isla Mujeres has plenty of other dives available. Blessed with a plethora of white sand beaches, the island is best known for the endless **Playa Norte** (North Beach) off Isla Town's coast, but a number of pleasant **beaches★★**, like **Playa Lancheros**, enjoy the calm waters on the west coast.

Getting There & Around

Airport Transfers – To get there from **Cancún airport**, take a taxi to **Puerto Juárez** or **Gran Puerto Cancún** (*15min north of ElCentro*). Express boats depart every half hour 6:30am–9pm; hourly 9pm–midnight.
The crossing takes 15 minutes, while the fare is $3–$4 one way/$6–$7 round-trip. Several companies provide pre-booked airport transfers, one way or round trip. They'll meet you outside customs, take you to Puerto Juárez, and meet you on your return trip (*Agi Tours*, *998-887-6967*, *www.agitours.com*; **Luxury Van Transportation**, *998-206-2526*, *998-881-7307/ 7308*).
Zona Hotelera/El Centro – With **Ultra Mar** (*www.granpuerto.com. mx*, *998-843-2011*) you can get to Mujeres straight from the Zona Hotelera's **Playa Tortugas** (*daily 9am–1pm, 4pm; return 9:30am–1:30pm, 3:30pm, 5:30pm; $4 round trip, 30min one way*).
Alternatively, you can take a taxi or catch the "*Ruta 13*" bus to the mainland port of **Puerto Juárez** where Caribbean Express and Ultra Mar's air-conditioned boats provide the faster service (*15–*

20 min, *$4*), and Caribbean Savage (*45–60min*, *$3.50*) the slower. The car ferry at **Punta Sam** (*get there at least 30min early; leaves at 8am, 11am, 2:45pm, 5:30pm, 8:15pm*), is five miles north of Puerto Juárez. Expensive, but fast water-taxis operate from next door to the **Xcaret Bus Terminal** and other beaches in the hotel zone.
On Arrival – There is a taxi stand to the right of the pier. Men with pedal cabs wait to help with luggage and to escort you to the hotels, most of which are downtown. You can also hire golf carts (*$15hr/$45day*), mopeds and bicycles. If you want to tour the island on a boat, these can be hired from the docks on Rueda Medina.

ISLA CONTOY★★

A pristine, uninhabited island covered in lush vegetation and encircled by reefs, **Isla Contoy National Wildlife Reserve★★** is host to more than sixty bird species, with thousands of seabirds and a great diversity of other flora and fauna calling it home.
Boat trips to this 6.5km/4mi island might include snorkeling on the reef, bird watching, hiking, visiting a museum and even a barbecue lunch (*see Nature*).

Getting There & Around

45 minutes sail beyond Isla Mujeres, Isla Contoy is best visited on a tour, available from any travel agent or hotel tour desk.
Prices range from $45 to $70. You could also try **Naviera Asterix/ Kolumbus Tours** (*998-886-4270*, *www.kolumbustours.com*), or
Sociedad Cooperativa Turística (*998-877-1363, Av. Rueda Medina, next to Mexico Divers*).

BEACHES

Cancún is known worldwide for its wide beaches of powdery white sand, which stretch 12km/7mi down its coastline. Despite the crowds and mega-hotels, you can still find plenty of sand to enjoy the sun and brilliant turquoise sea, such as at the northern and southern ends of the **Zona Hotelera★★**. *For beach clubs and bars, see Nightlife.*

ISLA CANCÚN BEACHES★★★

Cancún's beaches are at points 50 percent wider than they once were, following extensive restoration work carried out to remedy the devastation of Hurricane Wilma (2005). Today, the sands of Isla Cancún's beaches are a constant invitation to relax while watching the roll of the emerald waters. Cancún's beaches are found at regular intervals from **Playa las Perlas** (Km2.5) in the north, all the way to **Punta Nizúc** (Km21) in the south, providing a seemingly endless stretch of sun, sand and sea. Resorts dominate the coastline and often beach access is best done through hotel lobbies (every beach in Mexico is public access). The hotels spread along the coastline provide paying guests with palapa sun shelters, beach waiters, volleyball courts, restaurants, showers, restrooms, towels and lifeguards in addition to a variety of other services.

Bahía de Mujeres★★★

At the **north end** of the Zona Hotelera in the Bahía de Mujeres (*Bay of Women*), waters are calmer with good **swimming** due to the protection provided by Isla Mujeres 6km/4mi out to sea. The beaches here are more compact than the eastern coast's wide sweeping oceanfronts, but they are clean and the comparative lack of waves and current makes them more suitable for small children, with good swimming and water sports activities available. There are **water taxis** to Isla Mujeres from Playas Linda and Caracol, while a small ferry service runs from Playa Tortugas (*see Introduction*). Playas Linda, Langosta and Tortugas each have **diving** and **snorkeling** shops.

On arrival at Isla Cancún the first beach you come to is **Playa las Perlas** ('Pearl Beach', Km2.5), good for swimming, and water sports, with plenty of restaurants and bars. Further south at Km4, **Playa Linda** (Pretty Beach), has submarine trips, while **Playa Langosta** (Lobster Beach) at Km5 and popular **Playa Tortugas** (Turtle Beach) at Km6 are clean beaches with good swimming, water sports, restaurants and bars (*see Nightlife*). Small **Playa Caracol**, by the Xcaret Terminal, has a shallow sandy seabed, great for children but very crowded. It has restaurants, bars, and activities.

East Coast★★

Cancún's eastern beaches are less protected than those at the north end of the island, with more waves and occasionally stronger currents (watch for red warning flags). There are no beaches to speak of on the **Nichupté Lagoon★**, so most hotels face the sea.

Near **Punta Cancún★★**, **Gaviota Azul** (Km9), **Chac Mool** (Km10) and **Playa Marlín** (Km13) are good for relaxing, swimming and water sports. **Playa Ballenas** at Km14 is very popular due to the number of restaurants and bars. **San Miguelito** (Km16.5) has scattered Mayan ruins in addition to sand and surf, but **Playa Delfines**, at Km18 is probably the best on this side of the island, with a large white sandy beach and beautiful views.

At the southern tip of the island are a number of high end hotels and **Punta Nizúc** (Km21), an excellent beach with good snorkeling. In Cancún **snorkeling** from the beach is not that interesting, but it is good here, at the public area near the Westin Regina. One of the most secluded beaches, without vendors and loud music, is that at the **Dreams Cancún** resort; just walk through the lobby to get there.

ISLA MUJERES BEACHES★★

All of the island's good sandy beaches face toward the mainland, on the north, west and south coasts (beaches on the east coast are hazardous for swimming).

Easily reached on foot from the ferry and all Isla Town hotels, **Playa Norte** (North Beach), is the classic Mujeres beach—long and sweeping—but it has suffered in recent years from shifting sands. There is good snorkeling and scuba diving here as the sea grass acts as a nursery for young fish. The oval inlet of **Playa Secreto** at its east end is ideal for kids, while the palapa restaurants and bars keep the adults happy.

On the West coast, **Playa Lancheros**, **Playa Indios** and **Playa Paraiso** are popular, with palapa restaurants and smoking beach barbecues cooking fresh fish. Aim to visit these beaches outside of the hours when the snorkel tours are there and it will be beautifully quiet. Gift shops, bathrooms, chairs, tables, umbrellas, and equipment are all available.

Playa Garrafón at the southern tip of the island doesn't have a sandy beach, but it does have snorkeling and diving on the small, shallow, protected reef below its beautiful towering cliffs. The hefty entrance fee includes life vests, hammocks, kites, binoculars, lockers and showers (*see Nature*). There is also a 🐬 **dolphin swim** center here.

Playa Tortugas

© Ian Dagnall/Alamy

MESO-AMERICAN REEF★★★

Cancún is known for its diversity of **scuba diving**—from open water reefs to wrecks, caverns and caves. The coastline is characterized by pockmarked, jagged cliffs, part of an elevated ancient coral reef called "karst" or "ironshore." Operators take **snorkelers** and offer training programs for all levels of divers. Cancún, Isla Mujeres and Isla Contoy mark the northern extremity of the famous **Meso-American Reef** (*also see Cozumel and South*).

COAST

Four national parks encompass the main diving and snorkeling spots in the Cancún area. Off **Punta Cancún** at the northern end of the Zona Hotelera and **Punta Nizúc** at the southern end are national parks of the same name. **Isla Mujeres West Coast National Park** encompasses the area off-shore from Mujeres facing the mainland, while **Isla Contoy National Park** surrounds the entire island of Contoy. There are excellent beach dives and snorkel spots all along the coast, but most dive operators take divers by boat to the deeper dives and more interesting parts of the reef. The water is so clear that snorkelers also enjoy going out where they can see the rainbow colors of tropical fish and healthy corals, sponges and sea fans.

The best local snorkeling is at Isla Mujeres and Isla Contoy. There is great snorkeling throughout the Riviera Maya further south, but it is particularly good at **Xel-Há★★** (*see Cozumel and South*).

Most of the diving around Cancún is "drift diving", due to the often strong Caribbean current flowing north along the reef. Sites close to the coast are also affected by onshore winds. Water temperature is warm year-round, varying from 23–29°C/74–84°F in winter to 29–31°C/84–88°F in summer. Visibility averages 15–30m/50–100ft. The reefs in the Cancún area are not as healthy as sites further south and the strong currents at times require a rapid descent. The best local diving is in Isla Mujeres

Colourful coral reef around Isla Mujeres

© Isla Mujeres Tourism Board

West Coast National Park, but most serious divers head for the **Riviera Maya★★★**, **Cozumel★★** and **Costa Maya★★**.

Punta Cancún National Park★

There are six main dive sites in Punta Cancún National Park. **Playa Las Tortugas** is probably the best snorkeling beach in the bay. **Las Banderas** is a long, elongated shallow dive site, 9–12m/30–40ft deep, with star and elkhorn coral, large gorgonian fans, and a variety of colorful sponges. It has cut-throughs with ledges and overhangs where you'll find French angelfish pairs, barracuda and jacks, plus lobsters and moray eels. **El Grampín**, at medium depth, 12–17m/40–55ft, has a sandy bottom broken by small patch reefs with caverns and overhangs where trumpetfish, puffers and three types of angelfish congregate. It's close to three other dive sites: **Chuchos**, **Largo**, and **El Túnel**. The **Navy Minesweeper wreck** (**El Barrera**) was sunk in 2000 to create an artificial reef. It attracts large schools of fish as well as eagle rays. An intermediate to advanced dive due to the strong currents, depth ranges from 18–26m/60–85ft. Contents of the wreck are still intact and divers can

Learn to Dive!
The best dive centers tend to cost a little bit more, but are usually worth paying for. Some dive centers run one-day courses and resort swimming pool sessions. However, if you are interested in diving and can afford it, go straight for an open water certificate (approx. $350), which takes up to a week, with plenty of dives included. Dive masters and instructors should be PADI, SSI, or NAUI certified, while large beginner training groups are best avoided.

go into many rooms, but some just want to see the big gun on the bow. Nearby, at the same depth, is the **Anaya**, another intact, upright US navy minesweeper wreck sunk in 2000. Look for eagle rays, jacks and large hogfish.

Punta Nizúc National Park★

The **Punta Nizúc** dive site is a large patch reef at 23–30m/75–100ft, offshore from various high end hotels at the southern tip of Isla Cancún. A more advanced site because of the strong current, divers use the marker buoy's mooring line to descend and ascend. The site is also good for snorkeling and is pristine, with large gorgonians,

MESO-AMERICAN REEF

Underwater World

On many of the dive sites in this area you can see the following: sponges, sea plumes, sea rods, sea fans and hard corals such as brain coral, star coral, elkhorn coral, and staghorn coral. Discover amazing anemones with arms waving in the current and Christmas tree worms in a riot of colors. The reefs are home to starfish, conch, spiny lobster, groupers, yellowtail and other snappers, porkfish, bluestriped grunt, butterflyfish, angelfish, parrotfish in a variety of colors, blue tangs, filefish, cowfish, porcupinefish, hogfish and eels, plus bigger animals like sea turtles, sharks, barracudas, eagle rays and southern stingrays.

sea fans, and anemones. Look for small creatures here—seahorses, shrimp, and feather stars.

Isla Mujeres West Coast★★

There are more than 30 dive sites around the island, most of them on spur-and-groove reefs off the protected west side. There are also a few wrecks. Besides colorful reef and fish, you can see lobsters, sharks, dolphins, sea turtles, rays, barracudas and moray eels. If you're visiting at the right time of year you may see the elusive **whale sharks** (*Jun–mid-Sept*)—gentle giants up to 18m/60ft long. **Snorkeling** sites visited on tours from **Isla Mujeres** include El Farito, Sac Bajo, and Manchones, or you can snorkel on your own at Playa Norte and **Garrafón Natural Reef Park** (*Carr. El Garrafón, 2.5km/1.5mi SE of Playa Lancheros; www.garrafon. com; www.dolphindiscovery.com*). Garrafón's reef has suffered extensive damage from hurricanes and boat anchors. **Shore diving** isn't too bad at **Punta Norte** and **Garrafón**.

El Frío (Ultrafreeze) is 11km/7mi northeast of Isla Mujeres, sitting at 26–29m/85–95ft. It takes about 1–1.5 hours by boat to get there. The 61m/200ft hull, covered with sea whips and black coral, is full of silversides, snapper, hogfish and huge grouper. Nearby there's another wreck, **Chairel**, an overturned car ferry at 28m/89ft. Both wrecks can be penetrated by wreck-certified divers or those accompanied by an instructor.

Cueva de los Tiburones Dormidos★★★ (Sleeping Shark Cave), 21m/70ft, was first discovered by a lobster diver in the 1950's. It's a fascinating dive—the sharks seem somehow hypnotized, which researchers attribute to the bubbles of fresh water rising from the floor of the cave. Besides sharks, you might see turtles and manta rays on this dive.

Manchones Reef I (*depths range from 9–12m/30–40ft*) is a good site for divers of all skill levels and shallow enough for first-rate underwater photography. The magnificent stands of elkhorn, staghorn and brain coral attract abundant schools of snapper, wrasse and blue tangs. It is also a good site for snorkeling, and home to the **Cruz de la Bahía (Cross of the Bay)** placed there in 1997.

Diving in Cueva de los Tiburones Dormidos

Diving around Isla Mujeres

©Thomas Hurtado

Other **principal dive sites** in Isla Mujeres West Coast National Park include La Bandera, Faro Celerain, Media Luna, El Yunque, Hondureño, Cañoneros, Punta Negra, No Name, Gran Pin and Piedra Atravezada.

Isla Contoy Reefs★★

Ixlache (*ees-lah-chayss*), off the south end is made up of large elkhorn and brain coral. The shallow reef has excellent diving and snorkeling. The **Vista de Mantas** dive site sits at about the middle of the island, on the west coast. Largely sand, it's a perfect home for southern stingrays.

CONTACTS

Cancún

Aquaworld – *Blvd. Kukulcán, Km15.2. 998-848-8327. www.aqua world.com.mx.* Probably the largest dive operator in Cancún and a five star PADI center, Aquaworld is just across from the Meliá Cancún. The center runs dive courses at major resorts, diving tours and also does dives from a man-made platform dubbed 'Paradise Island'. The company also owns the Sub See Explorer, a faux submarine glass-bottom boat that tours the reefs.

Manta Divers – *Blvd. Kukulcán, Km6.5, Playa Tortugas, 998-849-4050. www.mantadivers.com.*
Scuba Cancún – *Blvd. Kukulcán, Km5. 998-849-750. www.scubacancun.com.mx.*
Blue Peace Diving – *18 Calle Toronja. 998-887-3414/8069. www.bluepeacediving.com.*
Solo Buceo – *Dreams Cancún Resort & Spa, Blvd. Kukulcán, Km9.5. 998-848-7070. www.solobuceo.com.*
BOB Cancún – *Terminal Marítima "El Embarcadero", Blvd.Kukulcán Km4.5. Departures 9am, 11:30am, 2pm, 4:30pm (summer only). 998-849-4440.* Explore natural reefs, plants and marine life on your own personal submarine, BOB, a 'breathing observation bubble'.

Isla Mujeres

Aqua Adventures – *Center of town, Calle Hidalgo, in Plaza Almendros Local #10, across the street from Chili Locos. 998-877-1615, www. diveislamujeres.com.* An International PADI Resort facility with day and evening snorkeling and diving tours, plus beginner to advanced dive courses. Check their website for schedule and prices.
Bahía Dive Shop – *166 Av. Rueda Medina. 998-877-0340.*
Mundaca Divers – *10 Madero. 998-877-0607.*

NATURE

Outside of the treasures of the deep (*see Meso-American Reef*), the mangroves of the **Nichupté Lagoon**★ and the natural environments of **Isla Mujeres**★★ and **Isla Contoy**★★ provide a wealth of local nature to enjoy. Budding naturalists should consider a daytrip up to **Isla Holbox**★★ (*see Yucatán and West*), or down to **Biosfera de Sian-Ka'an**★★, **Xcaret**★★★, or **Xel-Há**★★ (*see Cozumel and South*).

NICHUPTÉ LAGOON★

Enclosed by Isla Cancún, yet supplied with fresh sea water by its two connected lakes, the serene Nichupté Lagoon is the perfect place to break away from Cancún's beach life. The lagoon's surroundings are full of contrasts; jungles and mangroves fuse with modern marinas, golf courses and shopping centers, with water-sports and sailing companies cruising the waters. These same tourist amenities brought landfill and sewage to the lagoon, which environmental agencies made stuttering efforts to rectify since the 1980s.

The lagoon system receives both fresh and salt water, ideal conditions for **mangrove** growth and a safe haven for several species of **fish** that inhabit the main body of water and inlets, as well as for the **birds** that migrate here yearly.

Another resident, the **blue crab**, comes here to breed (and keep the mosquito larvae at bay).

ISLA MUJERES★★

Isla Mujeres' **dive sites** are a great place for exploring the natural environment (*see Meso-American Reef*). Otherwise, the main places to see wildlife on Isla Mujeres are at **Dolpin Discovery** (*see Watersports*) and **Tortugranja**★ (*"Turtle Farm"; Carr. Sac Bajo #5, best reached by taxi; 998-877-0595; www.isla-mujeres.com.mx; 9am–5pm daily; entry $3*) in Laguna Makax, which protects six species of **sea turtle**. For eons these animals have come to Isla Mujeres to lay eggs. Sea turtles are still killed throughout Latin America for their eggs and meat, despite their endangered status. Founded in the 1980s by local fishermen, this

Isla Contoy

©Peter Maas/Wikimedia Commons

scientific facility has an educational role and welcomes tourists. An adult turtle can measure 1–1.5m/4–5ft long and weigh as much as 300kg/661lb. At the center, visitors walk through the indoor and outdoor areas where these prehistoric creatures paddle around in pools, separated by age, from newly hatched up to a year. Besides protecting the turtles that nest on the island of their own accord, the program also captures turtles at sea, brings them to enclosed compounds to mate, and later frees them to nest after they've been tagged. There's an informative guided tour and a small gift shop and snack bar.

ISLA CONTOY★★

More than sixty bird species and thousands of tropical seabirds live on this 7km/5mi long island, 30km/20mi from Isla Mujeres. Pristine and uninhabited, the island marks the start of the **Meso-American Reef★★★**. Isla Contoy is a **bird sanctuary★★**; species nesting here include brown pelicans, brown boobies, frigatebirds, egrets, terns, and cormorants. Flocks of **flamingos** arrive in April, while Jun–Aug is the time to spot **turtles** on their way to bury their eggs in the sand at night. Most visitors arrive on **tour boats**. The crew trolls for fish on the ride over and they stop to anchor for those who want to snorkel on the reef. Next, they pass close to the island for birdwatching before going ashore. Guests can swim, snorkel, sun, follow nature trails, and visit the nature **museum** (has bathroom facilities), while the captain prepares the fresh-caught fish lunch.

Flock of Pink Flamingos

©Bruce Herman/Mexico Tourism Board

The trip from Isla Mujeres takes about 30 minutes each way— longer if there are choppy seas. Trips also run from Cancún (45mins). The boatmen's cooperative standardizes prices; buy a ticket at the 🛶 **Sociedad Cooperativa Turística** (*Av. Rueda Medina, next to Mexico Divers, or at Las Brisas restaurant; $55 adults, $28 children (cash only) 998-877-1363*). Trips leave at 9am, returning around 4:30pm. When booking an excursion, always ask whether snorkeling equipment is included in the price, and double-check before heading out. Be sure to bring strong insect repellent, sun block, long-sleeved shirt and pants, head covering and closed shoes to visit the island.

RESERVA ECOLÓGICA EL EDÉN

Hardy explorers should check out the area northwest of Cancún known as **Yalahau**, home to a 500,000 acre research and conservation reserve established by leading naturalist Arturo Gómez-Pompa. Here you can explore wetlands, savannas, sand dunes and forest, learning about archeology, wilderness skills and animals (*$90pp; 998-880-5032 www.reservaeleden.org.mx*).

RUINS AND MUSEUMS

Cancún itself affords relatively few cultural options. The real cultural attractions are a daytrip down the coast to **Cobá★★** or **Tulum★★**, or inland to **Chichén Itzá★★★** and **Valladolid★★**. However, if you aren't inclined to take a trip into the Yucatán (*see Yucatán & West*), the **Riviera Maya★★★**, or southern Quintana Roo (*see Cozumel and South*), then Cancún and Isla Mujeres can at least give you a taste of what you are missing.

CANCÚN

Ruins

El Rey (*'The King'; Blvd. Kukulcán Km19, Retorno del Rey; 998-883-3671; 8am–5pm daily*) near the southern end of the hotel zone, between the ocean and lagoon, is Cancún's largest archeological site. The monuments of 'The King' were erected along the island's only paved roadway. You can still see a hint of bright colored mural paint on the facades. Take a tour or get there by local bus or taxi.

A couple of **developments** find ruins within their boundaries.

Yamil Lu'um ("Wavy ground") is a replica ruin where the Sheraton used to be, while golfers can get a dose of Mayan history at **Pok-Ta-Pok** golf course, which contains the real ruins of a temple.

Five kilometers (3mi) north of Cancún, **El Meco** (*on the road to Punta Sam; free on Sundays*) was a strategic commercial enclave until the arrival of the Spaniards. A small site, but in good repair, it contains the tallest archeological structure in the northern part of the state, a pyramid called **El Castillo** (The Castle). You can see the **Chakmo-**

El Rey

©World Pictures/Photoshot

Mayan Site Tours

Tours can be arranged from Cancún to some of the most significant Mayan ruins in Mexico including **Chichén Itzá★★★**, **Kabáh★** and **Uxmal★★★**.

Eco Colors (998- 884-3667; www.ecotravle.mexico.com) is just one of many companies that runs excursions to nearby islands, archeological sites, monasteries and other attractions. *See Yucatán & West, and Cozumel & South for ideas and tour operators, or book with your hotel tour desk.*

Ruins of a Mayan temple at the southern tip of Isla Mujeres

chuc Lagoon from the top. The site hasn't been open long, so there aren't any organized tours and you can enjoy it without crowds.

Museums/Exhibits

The **Museo de Arte Popular Mexicano** (*Blvd. Kukulcán, Km4.5, El Embarcadero Marina; Mon–Sat 9am–6:30pm, Sun 11am–6:30pm; 998-849-4332/5583; www.museo artepopularmexicano.org*) has over 3,400 pieces of popular art from around the country that you explore with an audio guide (Spanish or English). There is everything here from musical instruments to interesting tree of life sculptures illustrating Mexican themes.

The community arts center at **Casa de Cultura de Cancún** (*Prolongacion Av. Yaxchilan, el Centro; 998-884-8364*) contains a permanent exhibit of local artists' work and adds new items monthly, as well as organizing traditional dances, poetry readings, theater and musical events.

ISLA MUJERES

There are some remnants of a **Mayan Temple** all the way at the very southern tip of the island. Some think it was in honor of the Goddess of fertility, Ixchel, while others believe it may have been a lighthouse for Mayan sailors.

In **Faro Celerain**, there's a small **museum** at **Garrafón Natural Reef Park** (*see Meso-American Reef*) on the history of Isla Mujeres and the story of the Pirate Fermin Mundaca. Across the street from Playa Paraiso are the ruins of what was once a lavish home, known as the **Hacienda Mundaca** (*also called Fortress Mundaca; 10am–6pm*). The fortress was built by a pirate/slave trader who hoped to win the hand of a local maiden with whom he had fallen in love. He never recovered when she turned him down and married another.

Mayan Air Tours

If you fancy exploring Mayan sites south of the Mexican border, **Grupo Taca** flies between Cancún and Guatemala City, continuing on to Flores and then Tikal for $290 round-trip. The price for the one day tour includes all ground transfers, departure taxes, entrance to ruins, tour guide, and lunch. Get tickets through a local travel agent (*Cancún Airport; 887-4110, or 884-3938; www.taca.com*)

OUTDOOR ACTIVITIES

Except for the die-hard divers who never want to surface, visitors to Cancún might enjoy getting away from the surf, sand, and shopping. The golf courses here let you practice your swing in a unique Yucatán environment of mangroves, lagoons and Mayan ruins, while explorers of all ages will enjoy horseback riding through the surf, or cutting a path through deep tropical jungle.

GOLF

There are several golf courses around Cancún, with hazards that range from mangroves to Mayan ruins. Various hotels have special rate reservations, many also providing trips out to Playa del Carmen, just 40 miles south of Cancún, to play courses such as the PGA **Greg Norman** course, **El Camaléon** (*see Cozumel & South*). The most well-known golf course in Cancún is **Pok-Ta-Pok** (*Blvd. Kukulcán, Km7.5, 998-883-1230/1277, www.cancungolfclub. com*) on the northern end of the island, famous for the ancient Mayan ruins that act as hazards along the fairway.

This 18-hole, **par 72**, 6,636 yard championship course, designed by Robert Trent Jones Sr., has a magnificent view of both the lagoon and Caribbean from the various holes, plus various amenities to keep players comfortable.

Set between the Nichupté Lagoon and the Caribbean, the **Hilton Cancún Beach & Golf Resort** (*Blvd. Kukulcán, Km17, 998-881-8000, www.hiltonworldresorts.com*) is Cancún's only **par 72** golf club attached to a hotel. The 18-hole course's 6,767 yards of fairway wind through lakes lined with palm trees and birds. Formerly known as Caesar Park Beach & Golf Resort, the club and hotel are open to guests and non-registered visitors. The restaurant is also good for a quick meal after a round.

The **Gran Melia Cancún** (*Blvd. Kukulcán, Km12, 998-885-1160/1114, www.GranMeliaCancun.com*) hotel has a three-hole executive **par 9** 1,818 yard course with a magnificent view of the ocean, while the **Cancún Oasis Golf Club** (998-

Pok-Ta-Pok Golf Course

©Cancun Golf Club at Pok-ta-Pok

Mangrove canal at Trés Ríos

885-0867, _www.hotelesoasis.com_)
at the Oasis Cancún Hotel, has a
9-hole, **par 27**, 888 yard course.
The only **Jack Nicklaus** Signature
golf course in Cancún is found
back on the mainland, a short
drive from the southern end of Isla
Cancún, at the **Moon Palace Spa
& Golf Club** (_shuttles provided;
Carr. Cancún-Chetumal Km340; 998-
881-6000, www.palaceresorts.com_),
which has three nine hole courses,
each **par 36**, with a total of 10,798
yards through beautiful wetlands
and mangroves. The accompanying spa and restaurants are popular with non-golfing partners.

NATURE TREKS

Horseback riding past mangroves and through forest and surf
is a fantastic experience for kids of
all ages. One of the most popular
companies is **Rancho Loma
Bonita** (_998-887-5465/5423, www.
rancholomabonita.com_) 30 minutes south of town, which also has
wave runners and **ATV tours**.
Horse rides include a two hour ride
with soft drinks and lunch, or a five
hour tour (_$72, or double up for $55
each_), with a couple of hours spent
in the mangroves before arriving

at the beach for a swim and lunch.
You can even swim in the sea
astride your horse. Shuttles run
to **Cancún★★** hotels, **Playa del
Carmen★★**, and other sites on the
Riviera Maya★★★.

36 miles south of Cancún, past
Puerto Morelos★, **Trés Ríos**
(_998-887-8077/8078, www.hacienda-
tresrios.com; see Must Stay_) is a great
place for **horseback riding
tours**. You can choose where the
guide will take you: on a ride to the
beach, or an adventure through
the jungle, mangroves and lakes.
Trés Ríos also has kayaking, canoeing, snorkeling and cycling. Prices
include transportation from your
hotel in air conditioned vehicles,
entrance fees, buffet lunch, open
bar, lockers and towels.

Horseback riding on the beach

OUTDOOR ACTIVITIES

45

WATERSPORTS

Thanks to its beautiful natural environment with acres of coastline and a large sheltered lagoon, Cancún gives visitors a wide variety of water sports to enjoy. These include deep-sea fishing, waterskiing, windsurfing, jet-skiing, and swim with dolphins programs. Beach-side hotels usually have plenty of rental equipment.

Nichupté Lagoon★

There are in fact four lagoons sealed in by Isla Cancún, but they tend to be referred to by the catch-all 'Nichupté'. The largest is the **Nichupté Lagoon**, then the **Bojórquez Lagoon**, the **Río Inglés Lagoon** and the **Caleta Nizúc**. Each flows into the next and you usually can't tell which one you are in. Most tours of the lagoon are on two-person **wave runners**. Wave runners always have two passengers and guides may drive you, go as a passenger, or lead you single file in another wave runner, with another guide bringing up the rear to ensure no-one gets lost.

Marina Barracuda (*Blvd. Kuku-lcán, Km14, 998-885-3444, www.marinabarracuda.com*) runs two-hour wave runner tours, ending with snorkeling at Punta Nizúc. Fees start at $55, including equipment and refreshments.

Aqua Tours (*998-849-4748; www.dolphindiscovery.com*) runs jungle tours, navigating through the mangroves of the lagoon and snorkeling on the barrier reef. Take the 'Sailing Quest' to the Dolphin Discovery for a buffet lunch and time with dolphins, stingrays and sharks, or a sunset dinner cruise on the lagoon, with a wine and lobster dinner on a 60ft galleon.

Aqua Fun (*Blvd. Kukulcán, Km16.5; 998-885-2930*) has wave runners with similar tours and prices as those at Marina Barracuda. A two-hour tour of the mangroves costs $55, including snorkeling at Punta Nizúc. The ever-prevalent **Aqua-world** (*Blvd. Kukulcán, Km15.2; 998-848-8300; www.aquaworld.com.mx*) also runs wave runner tours.

Hire Your Own...

Canoes/Kayaks – The waters of the Nichupté Lagoon are calm, and a canoe or kayak is a perfect way to explore the mangroves at your own pace. Check with hotels or dive shops on the beach for rentals.

Windsurfers– With its natural cooling off-shore breezes, wind-surfing is very good in Cancún both on the Nichupté Lagoon and the sheltered waters of the northern Bahía de Mujeres.

Waterskis – Like windurfing, this is best done on the lagoon or in Bahía de Mujeres. A number of marinas provide lessons. Prices start at $70 per hour.

Nichupté Lagoon

©World Pictures/Photoshot

🐬 Swim with Dolphins

Swim with dolphins programs are increasingly popular in Mexico. It's a perfect family adventure and one of the best educational activities for kids. The programs are pretty much all the same, as are the costs, which increase with the amount of interaction with these intelligent mammals. It's a thrilling experience, even life-changing for youngsters; just make sure that you know exactly what you are paying for before you pass over your hard-earned cash.

There are three places with Dolphin Encounter Programs in **Cancún** alone, plus two on **Isla Mujeres**, two on **Cozumel** and several in nature parks on the **Riviera Maya** (see Cozumel and South). In Cancún, the best choice is the **Delphinus Dreams** facility in the Dreams Resort (Km7.5 at Punta Cancún). **Dolphinaris** is another program, at the Wet N'Wild waterpark (see below). In 🐬 **La Isla** shopping center, the **Interactive Aquarium** runs a swim program for $135. The price includes free admission to the aquarium (below).

Dolphin Discovery - Camino Sac Bajo Lote 26 (antes 96 al 102). Fraccionamiento Paraíso Laguna Macax, Isla Mujeres. www.dolphindiscovery.com. Toll Free: 866-393-5158 (USA), 01-800-727-5391 (Mexico). Part of a chain of dolphin encounter experiences run at different parks, Dolphin Discovery Isla Mujeres is run by the biggest dolphin operation in the thriving local market. A variety of packages are available, but they all involve kissing and shaking hands with dolphins as a minimum. The minimum program and the best one for kids is the "Dolphin Encounter" ($60-$75),

where participants can stand on a platform in the water and interact with dolphins. In the less expensive swimming package ($99; 8-year-olds and up) you ride on the dolphin's belly, while in the 'Royal Swim' package ($149) you are towed by their dorsal fin, before the 'foot push', in which you rise out of the water propelled by dolphins. Dolphin Discovery also runs the operation at **Garrafón Natural Reef Park** (see Meso-American Reef).

Sportfishing

Cancún and Isla Mujeres are both well-known areas for deep-sea fishing, which can be arranged at numerous piers and travel agencies. Prices range from $200–$350 for four hours and longer. Boats usually come with a captain, first mate, gear, bait and beers. Fishing is slightly better and cheaper off Isla Mujeres or Isla Cozumel if you head over there for the day.

Waterparks & Aquariums

Wet N' Wild – Blvd. Kukulcán, Km25. 998-881-3000. The only water park in the Zona Hotelera extends over 18 acres beside the Nichupté Lagoon, with attractions for guests of all ages, including a wave-pool, waterslides, the gently moving Lazy River that meanders through the entire park, and a Kids' Park for small children.

Interactive Aquarium –
🐬 La Isla Shopping Center, Blvd. Kukulcán, Km12.5. 998-884-8487. This aquarium has marine life from tidal pools to the deep ocean, including rarities like seahorses, tiger and bull sharks. This is one of the places to **swim with dolphins** (see above).

SAILING AND CRUISING

Most people that step aboard a boat in Cancún do so in numbers, surrounded by other tourists booked onto **pleasure boats** heading out to Islas **Mujeres★★**, **Contoy★★** or **Cozumel★★**. Yet the traffic isn't one way, as legions of tender boats spill forth from the **cruise ships** anchored off-shore, full of expectant passengers intent on exploring Cancún's coast, before heading deeper into the Yucatán.

Berths and boat hire can be found in the **marinas** along the Caribbean Coast—in Cancún, Isla Mujeres, Cozumel, Playa del Carmen, Puerto Aventuras and Xcalak on the Costa Maya—with more on their way. Strong coastal winds and a beautiful coastline dotted with bays, mangroves and white beaches provide good sailing all along the Caribbean coast, but facilities can be intermittent.

Boats at Isla Mujeres

© Bruce Herman/Mexico Tourism Board

Sailing Tours

Many companies run pleasure boat tours to Isla Mujeres from Cancún, whether it is aboard a motor yacht, catamaran or trimaran. They take groups of swimmers, snorkelers and day trippers on boats that usually include lunch, drinks (tequila slammers anyone?) and snorkel gear in the price, with a 9am departure and 5pm return.
Sea Passion (*998-877-0798, 984-803-0399; www.seapassion.net*) is a 75-foot catamaran that sails from Cancún to Isla Mujeres for snorkeling, shopping and lunch at a private beach club. The full

day tour, including food and drink, costs $79 (other packages also available).

La Pinta (*884-5333, www. kolumbustours.com*) is a replica of Christopher Columbus's ship, which departs from Playa Tortugas to Isla Mujeres (*Wed, Fri; $55*) and from Marina Hacienda del Mar (north of Cancún) to Isla Contoy (*Tue, Thu, Sun; $75; shuttle service*).

Glass-bottom Boats

For those who want to explore the deep without getting wet, there are a number of glass bottom boats available, each providing tours of the reefs (snorkeling is usually more rewarding unless you have small children).

The **Sub See Explorer** run by **Aquaworld** (*Blvd. Kukulcán, Km15.2; 998-848-8327; www.aqua world.com.mx*) is a faux-submarine, glass-bottom boat reef tour.

Yachting

With a number of new marinas planned or already in the works, the Caribbean coast of the Yucatán is the spot to watch on the yachting map.

Admiral Yacht Club – *Blvd. Kukulcán Km5.8. 998-849-5317*. Find charters for cruising and fishing. The fleet includes luxury yachts, express cruisers, speedboats and fishing boats, all over 38 feet and the latest models in their class.

El Milagro Marina – *Bahía de Mujeres. 805-698-8165. www.elmilagro marina.com*. Full service, water, power, internet, cable TV, security, customs & immigration service.

Puerto Isla Mujeres Marina – *Puerto de Abrigo, Laguna Macax. 998-287-3340. www.puertoisla mujeres.com*. Full service, charter

Enrique Lima's Marina

Founded in the 1960's before Cancún was even a blip on the map, this marina was the first in the Isla Mujeres/Cozumel area. The **Isla Town★** dock and island quickly became a sport fishing center and for more than 35 years has hosted two regattas including the Regatta Sol del Sol, from St. Petersburg, Fla to Isla Mujeres, and the Regatta al Sol, from New Orleans and Pensacola, Fla, to Isla Mujeres. www.islamujeresmarina.com.

boats for fishing or sailing, alongside a boutique hotel at the marina.

Club de Yates (Yacht Club) – *Av. Rueda Medina S/N (near downtown). 998-877-0211*.

Cruising

It is usually about a 20 minute tender ride to get to shore from a docked cruise-liner, but the water is seldom rough as the sea is quite shallow. Cancún is a tender port and the ships anchor quite a distance from the tender pier.

Small catamaran on Cancún waters

SAILING AND CRUISING

SHOPPING

Cancún is a duty-free zone, but prices are high so the removal of tax charges doesn't always equate to good value. Crafts are of the production-line variety and the malls themselves are more like little neighborhoods with shops, restaurants, entertainment, activities for kids, and anything they can think of to keep you there.

The whole length of **Blvd. Kukulcán** is a shopper's paradise, with everything for sale at its landmark shopping malls, from the ridiculous to the sublime. In El Centro, **Av. Tulum** is the hub, while out on Isla Mujeres, most of the shopping is in **Isla Town**.

CANCÚN

Zona Hotelera

La Isla (Blvd. Kukulcán, Km12.6, 883-5025) is a semi-outdoor shopping village and entertainment center with over 200 shops, restaurants, and bars, set beside the Nichupté Lagoon. Massive canopies cover the streets running through the warren of shops, keeping shoppers out of the mid-day sun and focused on the next bargain. La Isla has more than 150 national and international stores, strewn around the quasi-traditional Mexican architecture. Bridges cross small canals here and

Local straw craft

©Bruce Herman/Mexico Tourism Board

there, while the whole development is ringed by an artificial river. The waterside restaurants are lively spots to review your purchases from La Isla's upmarket boutiques.

Plaza Kukulcán (Blvd. Kukulcán, Km13) might be the most exclusive shopping center in Cancún, perhaps even in the Riviera Maya. Surrounded by five star mega hotels, this mall has everything from fine gem jewelers to elegant perfumeries, handicrafts shops and designer boutiques, not forgetting the restaurants, cinemas and bowling alley. **Luxury Avenue** is a newer section of Plaza Kukulcán, showcasing world-renowned boutiques like Cartier and Louis Vuitton.

Plaza Flamingo (Blvd. Kukulcán, Km11.5, 10am–10pm, 998-883-2855, www.flamingo.com.mx) is a large mall, but looking a little jaded these days next to more lively rivals like Plaza Kukulcán. In the heart of the hotel zone, the Flamingo has a couple of restaurants and near 100 stores selling merchandise from beachwear to fine jewelry.

Plaza La Fiesta (Blvd. Kukulcán, Km9, 9am–7pm, 883-2116) just in front of the convention center is a vast handicrafts flea market. Be wary of glittering junk, but there are a few good items to be found here.

El Centro

Given the hotel zone's plethora of modern malls, not many people bother to venture downtown to do their shopping, but if you do, you should visit **Mercado 28** (*Market 28*). This typical flea market is Cancún's largest, selling fresh fruit and vegetables. There are also several restaurants for a quick bite or a cold beer, alongside lanes of souvenir and jewelry shops of varying quality. This is a good place to spend time polishing up your bargaining skills.

If arts and crafts are your thing, **Ki-Huic** (*Av. Tulum; open 9am–10pm*) is one of the oldest artisan markets in Cancún. It sells anything you can imagine, including traditional arts and crafts, clothes, jewelry and kitsch.

The biggest mall in El Centro is **Plaza Las Americas** (*887-4839*), at the end of Avenida Tulum, relatively close to the Zona Hotelera. The Plaza is home to El Centro's large department stores in addition to shops, restaurants, cinemas, and bookstores. Other malls downtown include **La Gran Plaza** (*Nichupté Av.*) and **Paseo Cancún** (*Av. Andres Quintana Roo*); both have cinemas and restaurants, in addition to the usual shops.

ISLA MUJERES

Shopping is altogether more relaxed on Isla Mujeres and the prices tend to be lower here, among the cobbled streets and short two-story houses painted in alluring Caribbean hues. There is a distinctive Caribbean influence in the wares on sale, from the neck-laces made of coral and sea shells, to the small inlaid boxes. However, most items on sale are imported from other parts of Mexico; from Oaxacan black pottery to sarapes or blankets from Saltillo, or fine Talavera ceramics from Puebla. A couple of art galleries sell local paintings and sculptures alongside foreign works.

Downtown, **Galeria de Arte Mexicano** (*Mon–Sat 9am–9pm, Sun 11am–5:30pm*) sells family-designed silver jewelry and handicrafts, as well as ceramics and hand-painted rugs from Oaxaca.

Karla and Maria Artesania (*Av. Hidalgo y Centro, Mon–Sat 10am–8pm, Sun 10am–5pm*), also in the downtown area, has clothing and handicrafts from different towns throughout Mexico.

If you would like to choose your own gem and have it set for you, try **Joyeria Maritza** (*Av. Hidalgo #14, Centro/Av. Juarez #7/Corner Nicolas Bravo, 998-877-1250*).

Artesanias Arco Iris (*Av. Hidalgo/ Av. Juarez, Mon–Sat 9am–9pm, Sun 9am–5pm*) sells silver, stones, handicrafts, carved boxes and blankets.

How Much Did You Say?
Shopping can be a great experience if you go out with the right attitude. Outside of the high rent shops, vendors expect you to bargain. They always give a price about two thirds higher than they think they will get. Even if you think the price is reasonable compared to home, it is worth engaging in bargaining; vendors tend to respect a hard (but polite) bargainer.

KIDS

Cancún and the Yucatán are perfect destinations to take children and young people. Many hotels have daily programs for kids and teens that keep them from getting bored. So many activities and sightseeing spots are educational here that kids often don't realize they are learning! From the animal kingdom and conservation to the mystic history of the Maya and the brash adventures of the conquistadors, they'll come back with plenty to talk about at school.

The endless **beaches★★★** (see Beaches), **resorts** (see Must Stay) and **watersports** (see Watersports) in Cancún could keep families occupied for weeks, but there's much more to see. **Swimming with dolphins** is a rare, possibly once-in-a-lifetime opportunity kids will never forget, with plenty of places to do it in and around Cancún (see Watersports).

Kayaking on the Nichupté Lagoon (see Watersports), going on a **mangrove/jungle trek**, horseback ride, **ATV tour** (see Outdoor Activities), or **boat expedition** to Isla Contoy, are all wonderful introductions to an animal kingdom the like of which many kids will not have seen before (see Nature). Children over 12 can try **scuba diving**, but younger kids can simply don a mask and **snorkel**

to see the area's beautiful sea life and reefs (see Meso-American Reef). **Glass-bottom boats** (see Sailing and Cruising) are a perfect way to bring the underwater world to life for younger children. Fans of **water parks** should visit Wet 'n Wild (see Watersports).

The giant **Mayan ruins** of the Yucatán will take you on thrilling adventures (get a guide who knows his stuff, or read up in advance) further down the Riviera at scenic **Tulum★★** and atmospheric **Cobá★★** (see Cozumel and South), or north at the most famous site of all, **Chichén Itzá★★★** (see Yucatán and West).

Snorkeling the beautiful cenotes and rivers at **Xcaret★★★** and **Xel-Há★★** on the **Riviera★★★** is probably one of the best family fun daytrips from Cancún (see Cozumel and South).

Family on a banana boat ride in the lagoon

©Nadine Markova/Mexico Tourism Board

RELAX

The very same beaches that frequently fill with frenetic vacationers and activities are also restful places for relaxing, meditating and practicing yoga at sunrise and sunset. Many hotels, resorts and day spas surpass expectations with their relaxation recipes. With all the outstanding spas—and most having their own "signature" treatments—it's sometimes hard to choose.

Le Meridien Cancún – *Km14, Retorno del Rey, lot 31-1.* 15,000 sq m/161,000sq ft of European-style gardens and facilities, with separate areas for men and women. Both areas include hot water tubs, cold-water Jacuzzis, aromatherapy and hydrotherapy services, saunas, and 14 massage rooms.

Dreams Cancún Spa – *Punta Cancún s/n, Zona Hotelera. 998-848-7000. www.dreams.com.* The combination of dark wood and white accents at this spa give it an Indonesian feel. Whirlpool, plunge pools, hydrotherapy, cleansing saunas, steam baths, Vichy, Swiss and other invigorating showers.

Nichupté Destination Holistic Spa – *Blvd. Kukulcán, Km3 Esq Galeon.* Built on Cancún's Nichupté Lagoon in the style of a Mexican village, this spa hotel has luxuriant gardens, gymnasiums, saunas and steam baths, and plenty of spa treatments.

Isla Mujeres

Hotel Rolandi Thalasso Spa – *Fracc. Laguna Mar SM. 7 Mza. 75 Lotes 15 y 16, Carr. Sac-Bajo. 998-999-2000.* This Swiss-owned spa specializes in marine treatments, such as seaweed, sand and mud. Therapies can include external applications, footbaths, balneotherapy (a special type of bathtub), and massage in or under the water.

Spa at the Ritz Carlton Playa Mujeres (see Resorts)

©Ritz Carlton, Cancún

Spa Diamante – *Av. Hidalgo No. 6 (Downtown). 998 877 1432.* Extensive menu of treatments including aromatherapy salt scrub, cellulite firming, massage, facial, manicure/pedicure and body wraps.

Spa Izel – *In the newly opened Unik Island Resort & Spa.* US/CAN Toll-free: 877-888-8645. Treatments here are inspired by Mayan culture and other traditions melded with modern techniques.

Spa Zenter – *In Casa de los Sueños, Carr. el Garrafón Fracc. Turquesa lote 9 A y B. 998-877-0651; International: 1-866-705-1691. www.casadelos suenosresort.com.* Spa Zenter blends East and West, fusion and flavor, rituals, massages, body treatments, wraps, and facial masks based on fruits, herbs and natural essences. Massages here range from traditional Swedish to Ananda Holistic, "design your own massage" and reflexology. Facials, manicures, pedicures and yoga (three times a week).

COZUMEL AND SOUTH

Cozumel★★ is one of the world's premier scuba diving destinations and an enchanting place to experience the essence of Mexico. Visitors enjoy Cozumel's beaches, nature and Mayan heritage against the surreal backdrop of the comings and goings of colossal cruise ships. Only 20km/12mi off the Yucatán Peninsula and 46km/28mi long by 17km/10mi wide, the ongoing growth and major modernization since the devastation of Hurricane Wilma in 2005 will come as quite a surprise to returning travelers. On the mainland south of Cozumel await the **beaches★★★** and ruins of the **Riviera Maya★★★** (**Puerto Morelos★** to **Tulum★★**) and **Costa Maya★★** (Tulum to **Chetumal★**), the wildernesses of the **Calakmul★** and **Sian-Ka'an★★** Biospheres, and the Mayan hinterland of the **Río Bec★★**, deep in the forest's emerald embrace.

Throughout this developing region, new Mayan sites are continually being discovered and excavated, while new tourism infrastructure, hotel options, flights, attractions, and beautifi-

COZUMEL AND SOUTH

Central Vallarta ○ 〒 ☆ Crococún
　　　　　　　　　　　　○ **Puerto Morelos★**
　　○ Victoria　　　　　　Yalal Ché
San Juan de Dios ○
★★Playa del Carmen ○ **Punta Bete**
Xcaret (Polé)★ ☆ **Punta Molas**
Paamul ○ **Xcaret★★★**
Puerto Aventuras ○ **★San Miguel** **COZUMEL ★★**
★★Cobá Xpu-Há ○ **★Chankanaab NP** **San Gervasio ★**
★Akumal El Cedral ○ **Punta Morena** ★
Xcacel ○ **★Xel-Há★★** **Punta Chiqueros** ★
Dos Ojos Cenote ★★★ Tankah○ **Tankah** Tumba del Caracol ★
Cenote Aktun-Há● **Faro Celarain★★**
★★Gran Cenote Tulúm ○ **Punta Tul** **RIVIERA MAYA**
Tulúm ○ **Tulúm★★**

Quintana Roo
San Ramón ○ **Muyil★** Laguna Campechén
Chunyaxche ○
Chumpón ○
★Boca Paila
Laguna San Felipe
Punta Xamach
Punta Conoco
Vigía Chico **★Punta Allen**
Cayo Culebra ★
Bahía de ★★
Felipe Carrillo Puerto ○ Ascensión **Punta Pájaros**
Chankan-Veracruz ○ Península Vigía **Punta Piedra**
Grande Punta Santa Rosa
★★Reserva Punta Nilul
de la Isla Chal
Biósfera Bahía del **Punta Herrero**
Sian Ka'an Espíritu
Santo
Laguna de
Mosquitos
Punta Pulticub

Los Limones ○ **El Uvero**
Punta Gruesa
Placer **Lago Uvero**
Punta Changuay

CARIBBEAN
SEA

Puerto Bravo
Punta Río Indio
Mahahual **Cayo Norte**
Punta Kanecaxh
Cayo
Punta **Centro**
Herradura
Banco
Punta Xcava **Chinchorro★★★**
BAHÍA
CHETUMAL **Cayo Lobos**
Cayo de
Blackford **COZUMEL AND SOUTH**
Xcalak 0　　　　　　50km
Cayo
Chelém

cation projects continue apace. Accommodations and restaurants run the gamut from low key, homey inns to resplendent resorts providing a sybarite's dream. Indeed, the Riviera Maya is turning into an extended "Zona Hotelera"

(*see Cancún*), as its miles of once-empty beaches are gradually peppered with mega-resorts. Tourism along the Costa Maya is still a few years behind **Cancún★★**, but its dazzling beauty, Mayan sites and position as the gateway to Belize,

Scuba diving, Isla Cozumel

©Cozumel Promotion Board

relentlessly drive development, Cancún style, all along the coast.

ISLA COZUMEL★★

Mexico's largest Caribbean island sits on the **Meso-American Reef★★★** (also known as the Great Mayan Reef), the second largest in the world, set offshore from Playa del Carmen and the Yucatán Peninsula. Surrounded by coral reefs and transparent waters, Cozumel has excellent beaches, scuba diving and snorkeling.

Getting There & Around

Vacationers can fly direct (see infobox, right) to **Cozumel Airport**, or transfer from Cancún airport. From **Cancún Airport** you could also travel to **Playa del Carmen** by bus (about $8.50) or taxi (about $30 for 4–5 people), then take one of the **passenger ferries**. The ferries take 45 minutes and are operated by two competing companies (tickets not transferable; $14 one way/$20 round trip): Mexico Waterjets (6am–9pm; 987-872-

1508) and Ultra Mar (6am–11pm; 984-803-5581). The **car ferry** runs from Punta Venado (Calico): 987 872 7688, www.transcaribemex.com.

San Miguel★

The only real town on Cozumel, San Miguel has shopping, entertainment, a museum, and excellent people watching in a quieter environment than Cancún. The **Playa del Carmen★★** ferries dock here, and from Playa you can take a bus to **Cancún★★, Tulum★★, Xcaret★★★, Xel-Há★★** and other places on the peninsula. Only a short distance from one of the world's busiest cruise ship piers, the large main square (**The Plaza**) and the blocks surrounding it are full of shops selling jewelry, T-shirts, Mexican and Mayan decorations and souvenirs, great restaurants, banks (with ATMs), pharmacies, dive shops, small hotels, plus a local market selling handicrafts, leather and silver. **Avenida Rafael Melgar★** (also called the **Malecon★**) runs

Plaza Festivities

Be sure to visit the square Sunday evenings when everyone (including local families with members from great grandparents to babes in arms) comes out to enjoy the fun, fiesta atmosphere and dance to live music.

along the waterfront and becomes **Carretera Sur** south of town. As part of the downtown renewal program, sidewalks were repaved and widened to create a more pedestrian-friendly and wheel-chair-accessible environment. The additional sidewalk space also invites outdoor dining.

West Coast★★

Outside of San Miguel, most **beaches** (see Beaches), **hotels** (see Must Stay), **restaurants** (see Must Eat) and the island's celebrated **scuba** and **snorkeling** (see Meso-American Reef) are on the west coast, the calm Caribbean side of the island that faces the reef and mainland. This is also home to **Chankanaab National Park★★** (10km/6mi south of San Miguel; open daily 7am–5pm; $16/$8 (ages 3–11); 987-872-9760), which encompasses Chankanaab lagoon, unique for its accessibility straight from land. Chankanaab is ideal for snorkeling and scuba diving among teeming tropical fish, or seeing the reef using snuba or sea trek. The large park includes the lagoon (a natural aquarium), dolphin areas and displays, botanical gardens, a replica of a Mayan village, clean and modern facilities, restaurant and snack bars, and, of course, a pristine beach. One of the main attractions is the **swim with dolphins** program.

South Coast★★

Formerly Punta Sur Ecological Reserve, **Faro Celarain Eco Park★★** (see Nature and Cenotes) was once home to a solitary lighthouse keeper. The park is made up of different ecosystems—the coastal wetlands, swamps where you can

see crocodiles loafing in the mud, and lagoons. In the latter eco-system a naturalist takes visitors on a boat ride through the once healthy mangroves damaged by Hurricane Wilma, pointing out interesting flora and fauna (spot the crocodiles). Also within the 247-acre reserve is an old **lighthouse** (faro means 'lighthouse') which has been turned into a museum, and **El Caracol** Mayan ruin. See Beaches; Nature and Cenotes.

East Coast★★

East of San Miguel is **San Gervasio★** archeological site (see Mayan Cities) and the road to the wild east coast, home to one basic eco-hotel and a good restaurant, Coconuts, plus several beach restaurant/bars scattered along the long, white sand shoreline (see Beaches). The coast faces the open sea and there is usually big surf and a strong undertow close to shore. Swimming is not advised where there is no lifeguard.

El Castillo, Tulum

©Stanley Rippel/Bigstockphoto.com

Exploring Cozumel

You can spend endless days on the island just relaxing on the beaches, exploring the reefs and trying out myriad watersports and outdoor activities. **Faro Celarain★★**, **San Miguel★** and **Chankanaab★★** all provide enough diversion for a day or more. Spend a day **exploring the island** in a rental car, on a scooter, or on an organized tour. Starting in San Miguel, take Carr. Transversal east and turn left at km7.5 for **San Gervasio★** archeological site. Once you have seen the ruins, continue on the Carr. Transversal for another 3km until the road arrives at the east coast. Turn right and stop at a beach bar or restaurant for lunch. Now head south to **Faro Celerain**, before heading back on the west coast.

RIVIERA MAYA★★★

About 20 minutes down the coast from Cancún Airport (*36km/22mi south*), **Puerto Morelos★** is a tranquil village popular with expatriates, who have gradually set up local businesses. The sleepy fishing village is slowly being replaced by mega all-inclusive resorts, but it's still much more laid back than Cancún or Playa Del Carmen. The area has an abundance of nearby cenotes (*see Nature and Cenotes*), a coral reef close to shore (*see Meso-American Reef*) in calm water (good for diving and snorkeling), while local mangroves are home to about forty bird species (*see Nature and Cenotes for details of Selvática, a local adventure tour company*). Further south, **Punta Bete** (*55km/ 36mi south of Cancún*), has a lovely, secluded "off-the-beaten-path" beach with a restaurant and a few bungalows. Just south of there is buzzing **Playa del Carmen★★** (*see Meso-American Reef/Nature/ Nightlife/Where to Stay/Where to Eat*), a port for ferries to **Cozumel★★** and a good base for exploring Riviera attractions. Playa was just a small backwater ten years ago and is now an important recreation center and destination in its own right. **Quinta Avenida** (*Fifth Avenue*), is Playa's 3km/1.9mi long pedestrian zone with restaurants, open-air cafes, and elegant shops. South of the ferry dock is a real estate development, **Playacar**, home to several resorts (*see Resorts*). Just south of Playacar is **Xcaret★★★** (*see Nature and Cenotes*), the original eco-park and the Riviera Maya's biggest family attraction, famous for its **snorkeling river** and the ruins of the Mayan city of **Polé** within its forests and gardens.

Paamul, an hour's drive south of Cancún (*16.5km/10mi south of Playa, before Puerto Aventuras*) has a good beach, perfect for camping, and a few facilities. Its main benefit is its proximity to the reef and its dive shop, making it an ideal stop for snorkeling or diving (*see Meso-American Reef*).

Puerto Aventuras, a private, gated community 20 minutes south of Playa, has accommodations ranging from top quality hotels to luxury villa rentals, and activities include scuba diving, boating, fishing, golf, and tennis. The community is home to a few small shops selling local crafts, plus a pharmacy, two small grocery stores, a shipwreck **museum** and the Riviera's principal marina.

Just past Puerto Aventuras, **Xpu-Há** (*'sh-poo-HA', 80km/73mi south of Cancún on Carr. 307*) is home to a beautiful, secluded, clothing-optional beach on a lovely small bay. Many think this is the best beach on the Riviera, but large, new, all-inclusives are going up and it won't remain undiscovered for long.

Beyond Xpu-Há, **Akumal**★★ has a wide half moon shaped cove and beach framed by a complex of tourist facilities. It was one of the first planned villages in the Yucatán. This is one of the top spots on the Riviera for snorkeling and diving (*see Meso-American Reef*) and is also home to turtle-breeding beaches.

Further south on the coast side of Carr. 307 is **Xel-Há**★★ (*'shell-HA', 122km/76mi from Cancún; 8am–6pm daily; $5; 998-883-3293; see Nature and Cenotes*), sited where an inlet widens into a natural "aquarium", with over 70 species and some of the best snorkeling anywhere. You might see dolphins, stingrays, or turtles. Surrounded by tropical forest and jungle, its list of diversions includes snorkeling, **swimming with dolphins**, snuba, sea trek, and exploring the jungle by train or on foot, along a well-marked 2km/1.2mi trail. Along the trail, visitors can see cenotes, grottoes, views of the sea, and diverse flora and fauna, including

macaws, water fowl, colorful fish and iguanas. Just outside the park, the **Zona Arqueológica Xel-Há** (*8am–5pm daily; $3*) displays the remains of an AD 300 to 1527 settlement where a sacbé (white stone road) leads to the House of the Jaguar, The Ramps, and to its left, a huge blue-water cenote. En-route between Xel-Há and Tulum is some of the best cave-diving in the world, such as at **Dos Ojos**★★★ cave. Other cave sites worth looking for in the hinterland include **Gran Cenote**★★ and **Cenote Aktun-Há** (*see Nature and Cenotes*).

Tulum★★, 2km/1.2mi north of Tulum town, is the only major Mayan site on the coast (*see Mayan Cities*). It sits on a bluff above a beach. Founded in approximately AD500, Tulum is home to the famous Castillo structure and the House of Columns. The picturesque site can be quite crowded, so access to buildings is restricted. Set in thick forest 45km/28mi north of Tulum on the Valladolid road, **Cobá**★★ (*see Mayan Cities*) was the northeast Yucatán peninsula's largest city for centuries until the city lost a bloody war with **Chichén Itzá**★★★ (*see Yucatán and West*). The surrounding forests are home to a great variety of birdlife, and Cobá itself is one of the few places where you can climb a pyramid, in this case the Yucatán's tallest, Nohoch Mul.

COSTA MAYA★★

The beautiful, unspoiled beaches south of **Tulum**★★ still attract environmentally conscious ecotourism travelers, but they are a secret no longer. A large cruise ship pier is already in use at **Mahahual**, with a mall and vendors already doing brisk business. There is talk of an airport being built in the next few years, but it is very controversial. The highway and roads are good, and nearby Belize ensures plenty of through traffic. Visitors have a choice of scuba diving and snorkeling on pristine **reefs★★**, deep sea sportfishing on the Caribbean Sea or fishing in the shallow flats of the unique salt water lagoons. Birdwatchers are dazzled by the bird populations in the mangroves and jungles, and several Mayan ruins were recently discovered in the area. Chetumal is the area's biggest town.

At the north tip of the Costa Maya is the 1.3million acre **Reserva de la Biósfera de Sian-Ka'An★★** (see Nature and Cenotes), a World Heritage Site that preserves almost a third of Mexico's Caribbean coast and a number of Mayan sites. Sian-Ka'an, translated as "Where the Sky is Born", has three core areas accessible only by scientists, while sustainable tourism is allowed in the so-called buffer zone. This vast area has a relatively small popula-tion, most living in **Punta Allen** or **Punta Herrero**. Local activities include tours, wildlife watching, fishing, kayaking, scuba diving and snorkeling.

Costa Maya

©Cenk Unver/Dreamstime.com

At the northern end of the reserve, a drive down the sandy coconut road (Four-wheel drive recommended) of the **Punta Allen** peninsula takes you past 50km/31mi of beaches, mangrove estuaries and offshore reefs, down to the quiet settlement of Punta Allen.

The gateway to the southern part of the reserve is the small town of **Felipe Carrillo Puerto**, made up of a gas station, bank (with ATM) and a daily market.

South of Sian-Ka'an, exiting Carr. 307 at the Cafetal junction (just after the exit to Limones), a road takes you to **Mahahual** (Ma-ha-wahl, also spelled Mahajual/Maja hual). This small fishing village has been transformed by promotion of the Costa Maya as Mexico's newest tourist destination, and by the construction of a cruise ship dock, bars and shops just .8km/.5m north. The sandy streets are being paved, and a *malecon* built along the waterfront. The hawkers, taxis and tour promoters come out in force when a ship arrives, but the village returns to its sleepy self once it has gone. Trips run to **Kohunlich★★** (see Mayan Cities) and **Chaccboban**, while Delphinus runs a 🐬**swim with dolphins** program at Uvero Point. Further south, the sandy palm-tree lined village of **Xcalak**, a deep-sea fishing and angling spot, is more or less the last port of call before the frontier with Belize at Cayo Chelém, the southern boundary of Mexico's share of the Bahía Chetumal.

The best scuba diving and snor-keling on this already stunning coastline of reefs and dive sites is found at the pristine **Banco Chinchorro★★★** (see Meso-American Reef), 48km/30mi out to sea. The coral atoll contains three islets, **Cayo Norte**, **Cayo Centro** and **Cayo Lobos**, and over 150 wrecks. Compared to other coastal reefs, the Chinchorro has been well-preserved, protected as it is by relative distance from the coastline.

BAHÍA CHETUMAL

En-route to the Bahía Chetumal, toward the end of Carr. 307 you drive parallel to the long, thin **Laguna de Bacalar★★** (see Nature and Cenotes) before arriving at the town small town of **Bacalar★**, made famous by this beautiful stretch of water and the nearby **Cenote Azul★★** (see Nature and Cenotes). The town is also home to the **Fuerte de San Felipe Bacalar★** (open Tue–Sun 11am–7pm; $2; 983-832-3600), a fortress built in 1729 in response to attacks by pirates and smugglers. The fort has thick walls, four bastions, cannons at the corners, high observation tower and a 4m/13ft moat. This is one of the few colonial buildings left in the state, reflecting the weak hold the Spanish had over this remote area. The **museum** inside presents a historical view of the region. Further on, past **Xul-Há**, Carr. 307 ends, joining Carr. 186. East along this highway lies the regional center and tropical border town of **Chetumal**, perching on the west side of the great Chetumal Bay. The town's bayside boulevard has several open-air restaurants popular with locals. The surrounding area has the most recently uncovered Mayan sites that you can visit, all set amid tropical rainforest. Chetumal's bay, where the **Río Hondo** reaches the sea, is home

to a **manatee sanctuary★**, and is a great place to kayak and look for turtles, crocodiles and a variety of birds (including herons, egrets, storks, ibis, spoonbills, frigate birds, kingfishers and osprey) on the way to **Calderitas** (north on the coast road), a popular beach with several good seafood restaurants. Out in the bay, **Isla Tamalcab** is a jungle-covered island lined with white beaches where the clear offshore waters are perfect for swimming and snorkeling. Local boatmen can ferry you there for the day (there are no facilities so take a picnic and whatever else you need).

RUTA RÍO BEC★★

Anyone looking for unique Mayan culture surrounded by lush tropical rainforest should head 124km/77mi west of Chetumal on Carr. 186 to **La Ruta Río Bec** (see Mayan Cities). This series of relatively unexplored pre-Columbian Mayan ruins is set in deep forest at regular intervals off the highway, including **Kohunlich★★**, massive **Calakmul★★**, **Xpuhil★**, **Becán★★**, and **Chicanná★** (see Mayan Cities). The pyramids display a unique architectural style (see Mayan Cities). Carr. 186 passes through the town of **Xpuhil** before arriving at the Mayan site of the same name and the **Reserva de la Biósfera de Calakmul★** (see Nature and Cenotes), home to the largest tracts of tropical rainforest in Mexico. From the Guatemalan border, up through the state of Campeche, this reserve is larger than **Sian-Ka'an★★**, at 1.8million acres. Over 230 bird species have been found here, while other fauna range from big cats and crocodiles to duck-billed tree frogs and anteaters.

BEACHES

The superlatives have all been used up on the beaches in this area, often a victim of their own beauty, bringing crowds from around the world.

COZUMEL BEACHES★★★

Cozumel is ringed by long stretches of soft, powdery sand, bordered by grasses and interspersed trees, quiet coves, cliffs and patches of rocky ironshore. The west, leeward side of the island has the calmest waters. Its beaches, set in sandy coves between limestone outcrops or on sweeping shorelines, are lined with **beachclubs** (each competing for the title of most kitchy) that charge beach admission, although buying food and drink may get you in free. Cruise ship groups take over some beaches, so watch for tour buses, or visit 9am–10:30am, or after 4pm. The less-developed east coast is less crowded and good for sunbathing, but the aggressive undercurrent is dangerous, so avoid venturing from the shoreline (not suitable for kids).

West Coast★★★

Distances listed are from San Miguel.
North of San Miguel are three good, currently free, sandy beaches. **Playa Santa Pilar** is the quietest (particularly the north

Playa Palancar

©World Pictures/Photoshot

end), while rocky **Playa San Juan** can be crowded, but has a nice beach bar and restaurant. Strong currents here push you out to the mainland, so snorkelers may prefer the beaches further south.

South of San Miguel there is an embarrassment of riches, starting with **Sunset Beach**, one of the three best snorkeling beaches, with a small patch of reef offshore. **Money Bar Beach Club** (*7km/4mi south*) is the second of the great snorkeling beaches with a small reef just offshore, but be careful of sea urchins going in.

Modern **Playa Uvas Beach Club** (8km/5mi; entry fee) on the old oceanfront road is well-marketed and busy but it has all the appointments and toys, and is near the reefs, with transparent kayaks for hire. Nearby, **Parque Chankanaab**★★ has a popular lagoon. **Playa Corona** (*14.5km/9mi; entry fee*) is popular with families. Carlos & Charlies Beach Club will waive the fee in exchange for bar orders. The 5km/3mi long **Playa San Francisco**, (*14km/8.7mi; fee $8*) is a big, half-moon-shaped cove with a nice beach (good for kids). The beach is close to the San Francisco and Santa Rosa Reefs, so dive boats stop here for lunch. On Sundays locals come here for music and barbecues.

All singing-all dancing **Mr. Sancho's Beach Club**, (*17km/10.5mi; no fee*) is very popular and has many activities (*see Outdoor Activities*), while **Playa Mia** (*was Playa Sol; entry fee*) is the ultimate cruise

Playa del Carmen

© Fernandomoz/Dreamstime.com

ship beach with lots of things to do. **Playa Palancar**, *(21km/13mi, then 1.7km/1mi to beach; no fee)* is natural, less developed, and laid back, with palm trees on the beach, hammocks and a good restaurant. The **Colombia Reef** and **Palancar Reef** not far offshore are among the best and most famous dive spots in the Caribbean.

East Coast★★

The east coast makes a great 🏖**day trip** and has long sandy beaches set in rocky coves accented by the occasional beach bar/restaurant. From downtown, take Av. Juarez east to Carr. Transversal and the ocean *(about 16.5km/10mi)*. Ahead to the left is the popular Mezcalitos Bar and Grill on **Playa Oriente** with hammocks under a palapa.

A 3hr drive further north (bring four-wheel drive, supplies and bug repellant) is remote and beautiful **Playa Bonita**, home to a Mayan ruin, and rocky **Playa Xhanan**. Back south on the paved road, continue to **Chen Río**, a popular beach with a protected swimming cove. **Playa San Martin** (was Playa Bonita) further on is quiet and uncrowded, before you arrive at **El Mirador**, a steep lookout rock. Lastly, just before you turn right

toward the west coast is **Playa Bush** *(AKA Bob Marley Bar/Rasta Bar/Paradise Cafe)*, great for chilling out with ceviche and a beer.

RIVIERA MAYA BEACHES★★★

Playa del Carmen – This sometimes crowded beach is long and wide with clubs, resorts, and palapas at the northern end.

Paamul – A little-known beach, Yanten, is sand mixed with rocky ironshore. Has a dive shop and restaurant.

Puerto Aventuras – marina community with beach and facilities.

Xpu-Há – Beautiful sandy beach with dive shop, accommodations and restaurants. Big resorts are starting to be built here.

Akumal – Miles of beaches over three bays.

Tankah Bay – The next bay and similar to Soliman. Manatee Cenote is nearby.

Soliman Bay – A quiet residential community with a long, narrow, protected beach lined with palm trees and other flora, about halfway between Akumal and Tulum. Good snorkeling and kayaking.

Tulum – The pueblo has wide beaches and higher surf; hotel zone beaches are well-groomed.

Xcacel – Turtle nesting beach.

COSTA MAYA BEACHES★★

Still the quieter part of the Yucatán's Caribbean coast, the Costa Maya is home to the former hidden beach jewels of **Xcalak** and **Mahahual**. These aren't so hidden any more since the construction of a large cruise ship pier at Mahahual and regional development plans. Enjoy them while you can.

BEACHES

MESO-AMERICAN REEF★★★

Just off the coast of the Yucatán Peninsula is the largest coral reef in the Northern and Western Hemispheres and the second largest in the world. Stretching 750 miles from **Cozumel** in the North to Honduras in the South, sections of the **Meso-American** or **Great Mayan Reef** are thought to be 2–4 million years old. Coral atolls, fringing reefs, barrier reefs, coral gardens, ship wrecks and warm, clear Caribbean waters act as magnets for marine life, divers and snorkelers. The peninsula itself adds a unique aspect to this underwater world, feeding subterranean rivers into the sea through its vast network of limestone tunnels and caverns (*see Nature and Cenotes*). **Banco Chinchorro★★★**, a large off-shore coral atoll, is a UN World Biosphere Reserve.

Reefs are marked on the map at the beginning of this section.

🤿SNORKELING

Some of the top snorkeling sites in Cozumel are at **Sand Dollar Beach**, **Chankanaab Lagoon**, **Money Bar Beach** and **Corona Beach**. Those on the Riviera Maya include **Xel-Há**, **Xcaret** (*see Nature and Cenotes*), **Akumal** and **Yal Kú Lagoon** (*see Nature and Cenotes*), **KanTun Chi**, **Dos Ojos**, **Gran Cenote**, **Actun Há** and many other cenotes in the region (*see Nature and Cenotes*), as well as off-shore at **Chinchorro**. In addition, many of the shallow sites listed in this section are also good for snorkeling and can be accessed with one of the diving companies listed at the end of the chapter.

🤿DIVING

Yucatán diving is usually drift diving. If you want to slow down, drop down to the sand and dig your hand in, but don't touch the reef. Successful dives depend on knowing what the current and tide are doing. The benefit of drift diving is that you exert much less effort as you are carried along. Just make sure you have a knowledgable guide, or do plenty of research beforehand if you are

planning on just going with a buddy.

ISLA COZUMEL REEFS★★★

Cozumel was home to a sleepy fishing village until 1961 when Jaques Cousteau declared it the most beautiful scuba diving area in the world. Cozumel has some of the fiercest currents of this part of the world, so most of the dives are drift dives. Visibility can reach 200ft/61m. Today, 30,000-acres of the island's reefs (85 percent) are protected by **Cozumel Reefs National Park**.

Many of the dive operators in Cozumel have been here for a long time and are very knowledgeable, but ask around if you haven't chosen a dive operator in advance of your trip. Hurricane Wilma destroyed much of Cozumel in 2005, when it sat over the island for many hours. The reefs, fortunately, didn't fare too badly, and, though the shallow reefs close to shore got the brunt of it, they have regenerated quickly and there seem to be more fish than ever.

Most of the dive sites are spread out along the **west coast**, and

around the south, but there are two superb sites on the northwest that operators rarely dive because of the very strong currents and washing machine-like action that can suck a diver down.

Barracuda Wall, ranging from 14–30m/45–100ft, is covered with healthy sponges, including huge barrel sponges, pink vases and large tubes. There's a good chance of seeing passing pelagics like barracuda and eagle rays. The other northern site, for experienced, very fit divers only, is **San Juan Reef**. It is covered with lush sponges and has some large coral heads. Depth range is 15–30m/50–100ft. Look for pelagics, morays and other species that hide in the camouflage of the reef, such as scorpionfish, lobster, octopus and seahorses.

The **Airplane Wreck** is always mentioned in relation to Cozumel, but it is a rather minor dive site in comparison to others. Thanks to the passage of 30 years and various hurricanes, there isn't much left of the small plane used in a disaster film and purposefully sunk in 1977. The site is directly out from the **El Cid La Ceiba** resort, in shallow water (*about 10–12m/30–40ft max*), and easily accessible from shore for both divers and snorkelers. There are scattered coral heads and some growth on remaining plane parts.

Chankanaab Reef is just off the ecopark's south end. It's an easy, shallow dive, 11–23m/35–75ft. Once again, the currents bring healthy sponges. Look for the two statues. Also at the Park's south end is a **cave** that's easy to find thanks to the huge number of silversides usually just outside. The thermocline will probably

hit you as you swim past. Max. depth is about 11m/35ft. Going a bit further south, you'll find the **Felipe Xicotencatl wreck** at about 24m/80ft. It's fun to explore the wreck but there isn't much sea life there yet. **Tormentos Reef** is one of the famous Cozumel drift dives. Depth is 9–21m/ 30–70ft and you'll pass over sand channels separating patches of reef decorated by varicolored sponges.

Yucab Reef, south of Tormentos, is swept by strong currents and has swim-throughs and arches to explore. Look for lobster, moray eels, jacks, squirrelfish, big coral heads and barrel sponges.

San Francisco Reef (*max depth 36m/120ft*) and **Santa Rosa Wall** are two of the reasons divers come to Cozumel—to fly over or along the reef with the current is exhilarating, or to explore the steep walls and their healthy invertebrates, which attract snappers, grunts, filefish, and angelfish.

Palancar Reef is the epitome of wall dives. Depth range is 5–30m/15–100ft and strong currents can whip up the action, but there is good snorkeling when they take a break. The spectacular growth is like a rainbow of color and the fish flashing by make it shimmer. Giant sponges are orange, yellow and

Colorful Palancar Reef

©Denis Sabo/iStockPhoto.com

brown, while multicolored parrot-fish, yellow and iridescent queen angelfish, red hawkfish and blue damsels change the color palette as they flash by. Palancar is made up of a few separate sections, called **Palancar Shallows**, **The Horseshoe**, and **Palancar Deep**. Sometimes turtles, sharks and eagle rays show up. Snorkeling is good at the top of the reef when the current co-operates.

Colombia Reef has two sections, **Deep** (sometimes called the Pinnacles) and **Shallow** (sometimes called the Gardens). You'll want to be a pretty strong swimmer when the wind blows from the south and the surface is rough in addition to the ripping current. Depth is 2–30m/6–100ft. Find large groupers, jacks and barracuda. The last three reefs, at the very bottom of the island, are the very best, but rarely visited. **Faro Celerain**, 24–40m/80–100ft, has a steep wall with several caves at 27m/90ft and a very large cave further down where someone could get lost in the passages without proper guidance. **Chun Chacaab** is 3–30m/10–100ft with a sandy bottom (before it drops away) where stingrays, goatfish and tilefish like to hang out. Incomparable **Maracaibo** is steep and falls away to the depths. Look for queen and French angelfish, wrasses, damselfish and chubs.

RIVIERA MAYA

Puerto Morelos National Marine Park★

The reef off quiet Puerto Morelos is Mexico's newest National Marine Park. Its proximity to the coast makes access easy. The water is calm and clear and good for snorkeling. Some of the species you might see are: turtles, schools of colorful fish, eagle rays, and several species of crabs and lobsters. There are a couple of nice wrecks too.

Playa del Carmen Reefs★★

There are about 13 dive sites near Playa del Carmen. You will find **bull sharks** here between the end of December and beginning of March. Bull sharks are usually found at 24–27m/80–90 ft. **Tortugas** and **Punta Venados** are the best dive sites. Other dive sites in the area include Cerebros, Los Arcos, Xcalacoco, Moc Che, Chunzumbul, Jardines, Sabalos, Barracuda Reef, Mama Viña Wreck, Islote and **Paamul**'s reefs.

Las Tortugas (Turtle Reef; 15–20min boat ride) is covered with coral and sponges where king crabs, nurse sharks, angelfish, grouper, tarpon, and, of course turtles hang out. The site has a flat bottom with scattered coral heads and sponges. Turtles are there all year round, at about 20m/60ft.

Punta Venados (*21–33m/70–100ft*), also about a 15–20 minute ride, attracts a wide variety of larger fish, such as nurse sharks, bull sharks, sting rays, turtles, schools of tarpon, and many other species. If you're very lucky, you could encounter a whale shark or manta, but it is rare. There's a ledge at 24–27m/85–90ft, covered with sponges and gorgonians.

Puerto Aventuras Reefs★

Just off-shore, Puerto Aventuras has a mild to medium current and three main reef systems, including a **shallow reef** (*8–10m/25–33ft*),

Reef and tropical fish,
Banco Chinchorro

©B. Jones & M. Shimlock/NHPA/Photoshot

a **middle reef** (*15–20m/50–65ft*), and an **outer reef** (*30–40m/100–135ft*), before quickly dropping to greater depths. Lush coral gardens, cuts and canyons range from 12m–39m/ 40ft–130ft. Hawksbill turtles are abundant here among the eagle rays, moray eels, lobsters, spadefish, and typical Carribean reef fish.

Akumal Reefs★★★

Akumal has several shallow dive sites. **Cuevas de Tiburones** is a reef with overhangs where you can find nurse sharks. Once covered by a lost fishing net, **Las Redes** at 12–18m/40–60ft has schools of fish, barracuda, stingrays, lobsters and occasional turtles. **Dick's Reef** has coral structures and channels that cut underneath, also populated by nurse sharks and barracuda. **Motorcyle Reef** has a 15-year-old, coral covered motorcycle surrounded by schools of fish, arrow crabs, and southern rays, as well as soft corals. **Yal-Kú**, in front of the lagoon of the same name has plentiful Elkhorn coral and tunnels to swim through.

Deep sites around Akumal include **Tzimin-Há** at 24–28m/80–90ft,

home to a variety of fish, sponges and the odd grouper. **Trigger Fish** (*18–30m/60–100ft*) have widely separated coral patches, while **Gonzalo's Reef** (*18–24m/ 60–80ft*) has large bright reef fingers and plenty of turtles.

COSTA MAYA

Banco Chinchorro★★★
Banco Chinchorro is the largest atoll in the northern hemisphere and the only atoll in Mexico. A Biosphere Reserve and surrounded by a National Marine Park, Chinchorro is located about 30km/20mi off shore from **Mahahual**, a 1–3hr boat trip. It's about 15km/9mi wide and nearly 48km/30mi long, consisting of coral reef formations covering approximately 144,000hectares/346,000acres. Open at both north and south ends, it forms a large protected lagoon inside the reef that's perfect for snorkeling. Because Chinchorro is so far from the most populated areas of the Caribbean coast, it has far fewer visitors, and is well known for its healthy fauna and flora, and over 150 shipwrecks (some are 500 years old). Typical visibility averages 30m/100ft, with water temps averaging 27°C/78°F. The water is so clear that snorkelers can see the shipwrecks, and several species of black coral at the bottom. Marine life includes 95 species of coral and over 200 different species of fish. Some of the tropical Caribbean reef fish you'll see include butterflyfish, damselfish, parrotfish and wrasses. Moray eels, stingrays, barracuda and lobster are also common, and visits by passing sharks, mantas, and whalesharks are always a thrill.

MESO-AMERICAN REEF

Costa Maya Reefs★★

The Costa Maya abounds with dive sites, some of which we have featured here. There is a medium current and depth varies from 10–60m/33–196ft. The reef close to Mahahual has fascinating finger formations with canyons and swim-throughs covered with abundant hard and soft corals. Nestled between cactus coral and ancient boulder coral, the plate coral is particularly healthy.

Sea Witch (*3.8km/2.5mi south of Mahahual; 13–22m/43–65ft*) begins around 13m/43ft and drops to a sandy bottom at 32m/104ft then drops again to about 47m/154ft. There are sand chutes to explore and sharks are regularly spotted.

San Antonio (*6.3km/4mi south of Mahahual, 10–30m/33–98ft*) slowly drops to 40m/131ft, with beautiful brain coral and gorgonians all around. A bit further south, **Grouper Point** (*16–30m/52–98ft*) is exciting in February and March when the grouper spawn; from about three days prior until three days after the full moon. It's amazing to see so many grouper assembled in one place, and chances of seeing sharks on this dive are high because the spawning attracts white tips and lemon sharks.

The wall drops straight down at **Río Huach** (*15km/10mi south of Mahahual*), with visibility around 100ft/30m. This is a great dive for fish spotting, including French angelfish, yellowtail snapper, and queen angelfish, as well as eagle rays, sharks, and an occasional whale shark.

Hob Ná (*12.4km/8mi north of Xcalak*) follows a wide canyon out into deeper water and at about 60ft/18m you begin to see huge grouper that seem to nest there. The tall, narrow canyons and large tunnels are great to swim through and explore.

Santa Julia (*8.6km/5.3mi north of Xcalak; 15–20m/50–65ft*) has massive tongue and groove reefs and deep canyons like city streets, similar to Dick's Reef in Akumal. The shallow wall and sand flats of **Doña Nica** (*2km/1.2mi north of Xcalak; 13–25m/42–82ft*) are perfect for instructing new divers. Large numbers of lobster and octopus make for great night diving. Nearby in deeper water are large tongue and groove formations populated by grouper and snapper.

La Poza (*.2km/.1mi south of Xcalak; 10–25m/32–82ft*) is unique on the entire Meso-American Reef. The box canyon style trench runs parallel to the shore for about .8km/.5mi. On one side is a coral wall, on the other a sand hill sloping up to shallow water.

1–2m/3–7ft tarpon, large schools of jack and snapper, and giant midnight blue parrotfish call La Poza home, as do lobsters, morays and scores of tropical fish. The dive usually ends at the "**Piedra del Mundo**" pinnacle.

At **La Chiminea** (*3km/1.8mi south of Xcalak; 25–30m/82–98ft*) the wall drops from 13m/42ft to 30–35m/98ft–115ft with sand flats extending beyond into deeper water. **La Catedral** is a huge cavern with a beam of light passing through a hole in the ceiling illuminating shiny tarpon, barracuda, and schools of silversides.

Other dive sites in this area include **Mahahual Reef** and **Río Bermejo**.

Cave diver? See Nature and Cenotes.

CONTACTS

Cozumel

AquaWorld - *Playa Paraiso, Carr. Costera Sur Km3.7. 998-848-8326, www.aquaworld.com.mx.*

Buena Ventura Diving - *US: 925-743-8844. 1 boat for 6 people.*

Del Mar Aquatics – *Casa del Mar Hotel, Carr. a Chankanaab, Km4. 987-872-5949. www.delmaraquatics.net.*

Dive Paradise - *Playa Villablanca, 602 Av., Rafael Melgar, Calle 3 sur, and Hotel Barracuda. 987-872-1007. www.diveparadise.com.*

Dive Palancar - *Occidental Hotels, 987-872-9770, ext. 8264. www.divepalancarcozumel.com.*

Dive with Martin – *Carr. Costera Sur, Km4.5. 987-872-2610. www.divewithmartin.com.*

 Scuba Du – *At Presidente, Carr. a Chankanaab Km6.5. 987-872-9505. www.scubadu.com.*

Sea Robin Diving – *Calle 8, Entre 5 y 10 Av., #140-A. 987-869-0833. www.searobincozumel.com.*

Puerto Morelos

Almost Heaven Adventures – *North side of square. 987-871-0230. www.almostheavenadventures.com.*

Marina Dive Center - *Marina El Cid, Luis Martinez. 984-807-9110. www.marinadivecenter.com. Dives led by author of books on the subject.*

Dive In Puerto Morelos – *#14 Av. Rojo Gomez. 998-206-9084. www.diveinpuertomorelos.com.*

Paamul

Scuba Mex Dive Shop – *Beach near Casa Willis. 984-873-0667. www.scubamex.com.*

Playa del Carmen

Abyss Dive Shop – *Beach at Calle 12. 984-873-2164. www.abyssdiveshop.com.*

Cyan-Há Dive Center –
Beach at Calle 38. 984-803-0558. www.cyanha.com.

Dressel Divers Club – *Iberostar Hotels, Quetzel & Tucán. 984-877-2000. www.dresseldivers.com.*

Phantom Divers – *1era Av. Norte x calle 14. 984-879-3988. 984-128-4210. www.phantomdivers.com.*

Puerto Aventuras

Dive Aventuras, *Omni Beach Resort, Puerto Aventuras Marina. 984-873-5031. www.diveaventuras.com. Ocean & cenote diving.*

Akumal

Akumal Dive Adventures – *Playa Akumal. 984-875-9157. www.akumaldiveadventures.com.*

 Akumal Dive Shop – *Playa Akumal. 984-875-9032. www.akumaldiveshop.com.*

Aquatech Dive Center – *Villas DeRosa, Aventuras Akumal. 984-875-9020. www.cenotes.com.*

Dive Ace - *984-875-9050. www.diveace.com.*

Tulum

Aktún Dive Center – *Av. Tulum, betw. Av. Cobá and Av. Escorpión Norte. 984-871-2311.*

 Halocline Diving - *Andromeda 4 (between Orion and Centauro), www.halocline-diving.com. In business 14 years; diving or snorkeling in ocean, cenotes or caves.*

Mahahual

 Dreamtime Dive Resort – *Km2.5 Mahuhual Coast Rd. 983-124-0235. www.dreamtimediving.com.*

Xcalak

XTC Dive Center, *Xcalak. 983-839-8865. www.xtcdivecenter.com. Xcalak to Chinchorro.*

NATURE AND CENOTES

The rich variety of ecosystems in the Yucatán Peninsula led the Maya to inextricably tie their beliefs to nature and the power of the natural world. This variety is best tasted on the Caribbean Coast where underground rivers pass through stunning **cenotes** before reaching the sea and its reefs. All this forms a 🤿 **snorkeling** and 🤿 **diving** playground.

ISLA COZUMEL★★

Cozumel's natural wonders are what first attracted the Maya to these shores. The island has several unique nature areas, including Faro Celarain and Chankanaab Ecopark (the land-locked lagoon has more fish than an aquarium). These parks have excellent modern facilities, snorkeling and diving. Cozumel has several **cenotes**, but they are mainly only for experienced divers. **Cenote Aerolito de Paraiso**, minutes from town is the largest (up to 3000ft deep) and is home to barracuda and sea stars. The sites of the **Riviera Maya★★★** and **Costa Maya★★** are also close at hand, and easily accessed on a daytrip or as part of a longer tour.

Faro Celarain Eco Park★★

Km27 on South Coastal Rd. $16 entry fee; free for under-12s.

Faro Celerain, once called **Punta Sur**, is a beautiful park at the southwestern corner of Cozumel made up of five ecological zones—coastal dunes, mangroves, reefs, lagoons and 2km/1.3mi of beautiful beaches. The park's coral reefs support a diversity of flora and fauna, while its sea turtle sanctuary does important conservation work and its shallow water holes accommodate submerged crocodiles.

Chankanaab National Park★★

Carr. Sur, 20min. 7am–5pm. $16 adults/$8 kids. See 'Introduction' and 'Meso-American Reef'.

Meaning Little Reef', Chankanaab has an archeological site, **museum**, botanical garden, good snorkeling and diving, beach areas, palapas and 🤿 **swimming with dolphins**.

RIVIERA MAYA★★★

Sights are listed North–South.

Puerto Morelos Cenotes★★

Just south of **Cancún★★** sits the tranquil village of **Puerto Morelos★**, located on a protected area of the Caribbean, the **Puerto Morelos National Coral Reef Park** (*see Meso-American Reef*). This is the terminus of the Mexican Government's **Ruta de los Cenotes**, which stretches to **Mérida★★**. The last stop before the Puerto Morelos area cenotes is **Dzitnup-★★★**, near **Valladolid★★** (*see Yucatán and West*). Along the road to central **Vallarta** there are many cenotes, such as **Boca del Puma**, which has its own eco-park (*Central Vallarta Rd; 16km/10mi from Puerto Morelos; 9am–5pm; 998-886-9869; www.bocadelpuma.com*) and **Siete Bocas** (*18km/11.1mi west of Puerto Morelos, then follow signs*). The latter, also known as **Deep Blue**, has seven openings into a connected underground waterway and was a Mayan offering site.

Playa Cenotes★

Cenote Cristalino and **Cenote Azul★★** (*15min south of Playa del Carmen; across from the Barceló Maya Resort on Highway 307, then follow signs*) are very large and quite deep, with clear water and good snorkeling, but limited sea life. Nearby is the **Chikin Ha** group ("Water from the West"), which includes **Kantun Chi** and **Eden**.

Xcaret★★★

72km/45mi south of Cancún on Carr. 307 to Chetumal. Open Apr–Oct daily 8:30am–10pm; Nov–Mar daily 8:30am–9pm. $65. 998-883-0470.

This beautiful eco-archeological park has cenotes, a subterranean river and enchanting beaches. Travelers can pause to catch a glimpse of colorful sea creatures or stroll around the botanical garden, the aquarium, the butterfly museum and the birdhouse. Additional **activities** (not included in the cover charge) include scuba diving, snorkeling, sea trek, Snuba,

©Mexico Tourism Board
Snorkeling in Xcaret

sky tours, **swimming with dolphins** and more.

The evening shows start with a Mexican *charreada* (horse show) at 4:15pm. The main show, "Xcaret Spectacular Mexico", starts at 6pm in a huge arena-like theater which is protected by a *palapa*-roof. The show includes a Mayan ball game and a performance of traditional dances from all over Mexico. In 2008 Xcaret added a 3,500 bottle wine cellar, exclusively stocking Mexican wines.

Puerto Aventuras Cenotes★★★

From Puerto Aventuras to **Xpu-Há** along Carretera 307 there are several cenotes, most with large entry pools making them popular with non-divers and snorkelers.

Cenotes - The Mouths of the Underworld

A cenote (*say-no-tay*) is an opening into the Yucatán underground river system, which flows beneath the entire peninsula. The peninsula was originally a giant coral reef that was exposed to the atmosphere millions of years ago when the sea level fell. Dissolution of the coral limestone created massive cave systems; many collapsed creating cenotes. Over the centuries, the rising sea flooded the peninsula's cave systems, leaving seawater at sea level and freshwater 'floating' on top. 'Cenote' is derived from the Mayan "*Dzonot*", meaning 'sacred well'. Considered by the Maya to be an entrance to the underworld, sacrifices and offerings were made in cenotes throughout the peninsula. In recent years some have speculated that the Maya inhabited the caverns when the sea levels were lower and that sacrifices were made to ask the spirits to empty the caverns of water again. Extinct fauna finds include the fossilized remains of camels, giant jaguars and mammoths. There are over 30,000 cenotes in the peninsula.

NATURE AND CENOTES

Haloclines

A 'halocline' refers to a vertical body of water that rapidly changes salinity with depth, as happens throughout the coastal Yucatán where underground fresh-water rivers come into contact with sea water. Light rays diffract when they pass through a halocline, giving fascinating visual effects, which are easily disturbed by swimming. Rock dissolution along the halocline can reduce visibility unless divers use special finning techniques to minimize disruption of silt. This is just one of many reasons why specialist cave dive training is essential.

Novice cavern divers should try **Chac Mool** (*100m South of Puerto Aventuras*), where the light of the sun casts a spectacular 'laser show' on sunny days. The deepest part of the site has a thick halocline (*see infobox*), which gives the impression that the surface is just above. A few hundred feet away is **Cenote Kukulcán**, accessed through a beautiful pool at one end.

The large, attractive **Ponderosa** (*South of Puerto Aventuras, not far from Chac Mool*) cave system includes the wide snorkeling pool of **Cenote el Eden**, where big rocks at the bottom shelter fish and plant life. The cenote connects to **Cenote Coral**, a photographer's favorite, through a long tunnel. 5km/3.1mi south of Puerto Aventuras is the **Chickin-Há** sanctuary, home to three cenotes, a zipline and cycling adventure, managed by **Alltournative** (*see Tours, following pages*).

Half a kilometer further south is **Taj Mahal**, good for cavern and cave divers, with four interconnected cenotes, an interesting halocline effect, and stairs to the water. North of **Akumal★**, **Yal Kú Lagoon** is a beautiful sheltered lagoon perfect for snorkelers. Just south of Akumal, the **Aktun Chen** (*984-884-0444; www.aktunchen. com*) park features walking tours led by informative guides of a spectacular underground cave

system (good for kids and older travelers).

Nohoch-Nah-Chich, one of the longest underwater cave systems in the world, connects with the ocean at **Casa Cenote** (*10km/6.2mi north of Tulum*). This is one of the few surface rivers on the Yucatán Peninsula. Both fresh and saltwater fish live among the algae-coated mangrove roots and rocks. The sides of the cenotes conceal small caves used by manatees living in the coastal river and lagoons.

Xel-Há★★

Xel-Há ('shell-HA') Tel: 998-883-3293. 122km/76mi south of Cancún on coast side of Carr. 307. 8am–6pm daily. $5.

An inlet widens into a natural "aquarium" with over 70 species and some of the best snorkeling anywhere. You might even see dolphins, stingrays and turtles. Surrounded by tropical forest and jungle, its list of diversions includes snorkeling, **swimming with dolphins**, snuba, sea trek, and exploring the jungle by train or on foot along a well-marked 2km/1.2mi trail where visitors can see cenotes, grottoes, views of the sea, and diverse flora and fauna, including macaws, water fowl, colorful fish and iguanas. Eateries include everything from fast food and ice cream parlors to bars and a few restaurants like the Caribbean, with a spectacular view, an International Buffet, and live marimba. Just outside the park, south of the main entrance, the **Zona Arqueológica Xel-Há** (*8am–5pm daily; $3*) displays the remains of a settlement that lasted from AD 300 to 1527. The main sights are: The Pilasters, a sacbé (white stone road) that leads to the House of the Jaguar, The Ramps, and, to its left, a huge blue-water cenote. Xel-Há ruins are unique as there's still an intact ancient cenote and sweat lodge there.

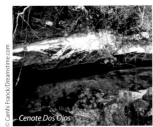
Cenote Dos Ojos

© Camhi Franck/Dreamstime.com

Cenote Dos Ojos★★★

1km/.6mi South of Xel-Há; 48km/ 30mi from Playa del Carmen; a 4km/2.5mi dirt road leads from the highway.

About 61km/37.9mi of the Dos Ojos system have been explored to date. The cenote is filled with rainwater that has filtered through limestone making it exceptionally clear. The system connects over 25 cenotes and is one of the longest known in the Yucatán Peninsula. The Dos Ojos ("Two eyes") of this famous site are two adjacent circular cenotes, known for their shallow dives, which connect into a very large cavern zone. Two different cavern dives start and end in the first 'eye'. The **Dos Ojos Cavern Dive** mainly explores the opening of the second eye, with plenty of light and huge columns and stalactites to swim round. The adjacent **Bat Cavern** dive is the darkest dive in the system with a series of rooms and passages. Nearby, **Hidden Worlds** (*on 307 north of Tulum; 984-115-4514;*

www.hiddenworlds.com) has exclusive use of a number of cenotes, with snorkeling tours guided along well-lit rope paths. They also run dives at Dos Ojos.

Cobá/Tulum Cenotes★★★

4km/2.4mi from **Tulum**★★ on the road to **Cobá**★★ (*see Mayan Cities*) is **Gran Cenote**★★ (*www. grancenote.com*), one of the most popular diving and snorkeling sites in the Riviera Maya. You can snorkel the huge cavern without ever diving underwater, while the accompanying cave system has good scuba diving. The cenote is part of the **Sac-Aktun** system and has white walls, crystal clear waters and impressive formations. The shallow areas lead to an open cave and a smaller jungle pool.
Cenote Aktun-Há (*"Water Cave"; 8km/4.9mi from Tulum*), once used for washing taxis, is a wide flat cenote encircled by trees whose roots plunge through the cenote's atmospheric underwater light. In warm summer months a five foot layer of algae grows over the water surface, while underneath the water remains crystal clear. Descending through the green mist you arrive in a surreal underwater world populated by fish and the odd turtle diving in and out. Not recommended for snorkeling.

NATURE AND CENOTES

Cenote Esqueleto (**Calavera/ Temple of Doom**; *2km/1.25mi from Tulum at the turn off to Cobá*) is not very good for snorkeling, but an interesting dive site, accessed by jumping three metres down into a pool, or descending a steep ladder. Formations in the cavern are dark, and there is a strong halocline (*see infobox, previous pages*), with plenty of light revealing fossils below.

Cenote Angelita★

Advanced divers must try 'little angel' (*17km/10.5mi south of Tulum; 984-151-9046; www.cenoteangelita. com*), which in fact is a rather large cenote that descends vertically for 200 feet. The first hundred feet is fresh water with crystal visibility, until you reach a dense strangely-colored middle layer of hydrogen sulfate. Bring dive lights, you will need them to get to the bottom. Go with an experienced dive guide and the correct gases in your tanks.

COSTA MAYA★★

Reserva de la Biósfera de Sian-Ka'an★★

10km/6.3mi south of Tulum on the path to Boca Paila/Punta Allen. There are entrances at Pulticub, Santa Teresa, Chump-n, Chunyaxch and Chac Mool. Guided visit (5hr). Tours can be arranged in many hotels at the Riviera Maya or contact the Centro Ecológico Sian-Ka'an (CESiaK) ecological center: 984-871-2499, www.cesiak.org.

The largest protected area in the Mexican Caribbean (6,000sq km/ 2,316sq mi), primitive Sian-Ka'an's coral reefs, tropical jungle, sandy grounds and mangrove swamps protect 23 known archeological sites (*such as* **Muyil★**, *see Mayan Cities*), 350 species of birds, as well as turtles, jaguars, monkeys, deer, anteaters and other endangered species. Appropriately for the carbon-neutral generation, this biosphere's name translates as "Where the Sky is Born". The area was declared a World Heritage Site in 1987 to protect the vastly diverse fauna and ecosystems. The reserve is thought to have been inhabited in the Pre-Classic and Classic periods under the authority of Cohuah and Uaymil. The northern part of the reserve has an ancient lagoon and mangrove channel trade route between **Tulum★★** and **Muyil★**. Sport fishing or sightseeing by motor launch is available by reservation from **Punta Allen**, a small peninsular fishing village (*see Watersports*). Guided walks lead further into the reserve.

Centro Ecologico Sian-Ka'an (*CESiaK; 984-104-0522/984-871-2499; www.cesiak.org*), a small ecotourism and education center, generates revenue through tours, fishing, accommodations, and activities in the reserve.

BAHÍA CHETUMAL

The great opening of the Bahía Chetumal was a designated **manatee sanctuary★** in 1996. The bay's complex ecosystem is home to 150 to 200 of these large aquatic relatives of the elephant. On the Mexican side of the Guatemala border, the bay is connected to the Caribbean by the Canal de Zaragoza in the east peninsular town of Xcalak. Nature excursions can be arranged in Chetumal, as can kayak rides through the mangrove canals and lagoons of the bay and the **Laguna de Bacalar**★★ *(see below)*.

Cenote Azul★★

At the southern entrance to Bacalar. Open daily 8am–6pm.

This very deep sinkhole, known as the "Blue Cenote," is so transparent that the twisted roots of the low surrounding tropical vegetation are visible. Its depth has been explored as far down as 90m/295ft; thus, swimming across the cenote's 250m/820ft-wide surface can be a daunting experience. A restaurant, a small collection of exotic birds and a handicraft shop are located at the water's edge.

Laguna de Bacalar★★

Eastern edge of Bacalar town.

Mangroves and palm trees line the banks of this huge 68km/42mi fresh-water lagoon. The crystal clear lagoon is also known as the **Laguna de los siete colores** (Lagoon of Seven Colors) because of the gamut of shades created by the variations in depth; the darker colors reveal the presence of the seven cenotes feeding the lagoon. A series of waterways connect it to Chetumal Bay and Río Hondo.

RUTA RÍO BEC★★

Reserva de la Biósfera de Calakmul★

52km/34mi west of Xpuhil, then 60 km/39mi south to Calakmul's ruins. Open 8am–5pm; $3–$4 (archeological site), $4 (reserve). No facilities, come well-prepared.

Covering almost 15% of the state of Campeche, the 1.8 million-acre Calakmul Biosphere Reserve is the largest tropical forest reserve in Mexico. At its heart is the vast **Calakmul archeological site**★★, only 20km/13mi from the Guatemalan border *(see Mayan Cities)*, while there are several other Mayan sites within its zone. Calakmul is home to many of the species of flora and fauna found in the **Selva Maya** (the combined forests of Belize, Guatemala, and Mexico), from big cats and crocodiles to duck-billed tree frogs and anteaters and over 230 known bird species. Logging, ranching and tourism is gradually eating away at this vast reserve.

TOURS

Cenote divers and snorkelers should contact companies listed under 'Meso-American Reef'.

Alltournative *(984-873-2036; www.alltournative.com)* has tours and activities to various locations, from kayaking and canoeing to snorkeling, cenotes, caverns, ziplining and bird-watching.

Eco Colors *(998-884-9480)* has several adventure programs providing once-in-a-lifetime tours like swimming with whalesharks, and guided wildlife safaris throughout the Yucatán, including **Yum Balam**★★ and **Sian-Ka'an**★★ Biosphere Reserves.

Selvática *(Carr. 307, Km321, 19km/12mi from turnoff, near the center of Puerto Morelos; 998-849-5510; www.selvatica.com.mx)*, specializes in zipline tours. Local tour operators include **CESiaK** *(see Sian-Ka'an, opposite)* and **Hidden Worlds** *(see Cenote Dos Ojos, previous pages)*.

MAYAN CITIES

The Caribbean coast is home to one of the most photographed Mayan sites of all, **Tulum★★**, whose famous Castillo is set on a rocky crag overlooking a sandy bay. The inland forests of Mexico's southeast corner hide a wealth of Mayan cities once far superior to this enthralling coastal jewel; from vast **Cobá★★** looming pensively in the emerald gloom, to the trail of sites along the **Ruta Río Bec★★**. Walking can be hot and the air humid among the butterflies and stomping grounds of elusive jaguars, so wear comfortable shoes, cover up with light clothing and carry water, bug repellent and a hat.

COZUMEL & SOUTH

COZUMEL RUINS

Cozumel's allure is its beaches and reefs, but it does have some vestiges of Mayan culture, and like **Isla Mujeres**, there is evidence from statuary finds that the island was dedicated to **Ixchel**, goddess of fertility, maternity, wisdom and the moon. At the heart of the island, **San Gervasio★** (*14km/8.7mi east of San Miguel; turn off Carr. Transversal at Km7.5, then 6.5km further; open daily 7am–4pm; $7/under 11s free*) was probably the core of worship. Built in two different stages—the Late Classic period (AD 1000–1200) and the Late Post-Classic period (AD 1200–1550)—San Gervasio still functioned as a religious site when the Spaniards arrived (16C). Visitors to the site will first see **Group III**, which includes the Plaza Manitas (Plaza of the Hands), home to the 'Temple of the Hands,'

Archway, San Gervasio

©Deanna Bean/iStockphoto.com

so called because of red paintings of hands inside. A network of sacbés (white stone roads) connects the site with the East Coast and coves where canoes once put ashore. Nearby, an arch protects an altar on a sacbé leading into the probable ceremonial center, **Nohoch-Na**, meaning "big house", where offerings were deposited. Another sacbé allows access to **Group II** or **Murciélagos** (*Bats*), which consists of a platform with the Murciélagos structure and **Pet-Na** (round house), uncommon in Mayan architecture. A further white stone road passes through to the Central Plaza, known as **Los Nichos** because of the niches decorating one of the structures. On the south side of the island is **El Cedral**, home to the scant remains of the oldest Mayan settlement on Cozumel (AD800).

TULUM★★

130km/81.2mi south of Cancún International Airport and 60km/ 37mi south of Playa del Carmen. Open daily 7am–5pm. $4. The 1km/.6mi path from the parking lot (parking $2) to the archeological site can be covered on foot or by train ($1). 984-206-3150. www.rivieramaya.com.

Templo de las Pinturas, Tulum

Tulum, which in Mayan means "wall," alludes to the fortification that surrounds the area, although its original name *Zamá* ("sunrise"), refers to the site's unique coastal location, perfect for watching the sun rise up out of the sea to the east. This location made it an important maritime commercial center and the site's archeological remains of obsidian, jade and copper testify to its trade with Central America. The archeological site was inhabited during the Late Post-Classic period (AD 1200–1521) and was one of the last cities to be built and inhabited by the Maya of the Yucatán Peninsula. The city is surrounded by a 380m/416yd north-south **wall** of three series, whose construction reflects the violent political conditions of its era. A thick outer wall prevented enemy access, and two inner walls separated the commercial and ceremonial areas. A 6m/20ft wide and 3–5m/10–16ft **wall** bounds the ceremonial center to the north, west and south. Tulum's eastern flank is open to the sea. A white sand cove nestles at the foot of the cliffs, where the trading canoes would slip ashore.

The site itself can be accessed from a narrow entrance on the west side. There are four additional entrances, two to the north and two to the south. From the wall, you can see several large, fortified watchtowers.

The site has over fifty structures, most of which are found along the two "roads" that run from north to south. Religious temples, tombs and official buildings, as well as residential platforms, originally occupied the area known as the **recinto interior**. More or less in the center of the city, in front of the Plataforma Funeraria, the **Templo de las Pinturas**(Temple of the Paintings), is probably Tulum's most interesting structure, featuring frescoes and a small altar. The lower level facade consists of four stout columns, large corner masks and three niches with sculptures. An image of the *Dios Descendente* (Diving God) decorates the upper level.

The largest and most photographed structure in Tulum, **El Castillo** sits atop a bluff overseeing the beach below, its entrance flanked by two columns that resemble serpents. Sculptures

MAYAN CITIES

adorn its facade, and the remains of masks are visible on the corners. At ground level, two small temples flank the stairway. From behind the sanctuary, a magnificent **view**★★★ of the Caribbean Sea unfolds (after exploring the site for a couple of hours, cool off in the turquoise waters below).

At the small **Templo del Dios Descendente** (*north side of the small inner building whose main monument is El Castillo*), the niche above the door houses a clear stucco sculpture of the Diving God, a figure with an upside-down head. It is believed that this god, who appears on many of the buildings in Tulum, was associated with the netherworld and the planet Venus.

MUYIL★

18km/11mi south of Tulum, on Carr. 307. Open daily 8am–5pm. $2. After visiting the site you can hire a guide on a 3hr boat excursion around the Muyil Lagoon, located inside the Biósfera de Sian-Ka'an ($10 entry fee).

Located only 15min away from popular **Tulum**★★, the archeological site of Muyil is wrapped in the thick forest of the **Biósfera de Sian-Ka'An**★★ (*see Nature and Cenotes*), providing a taste of the larger sites, like Cobá, lost in deep inland forest.

On the banks of the beautiful Muyil Lagoon, this 450ha/1,112-acre site shows evidence of human occupation from as early as 300 BC, but it did not reach its zenith until the Late Classic period (AD 600–900).

The site's tallest structure is **El Castillo**, a temple of six layered sections dedicated to Ixchel. Nearly 300 jade figures, all of them offerings to Ixchel, were found inside the building in 1997. Some of these offerings may have been brought here by sea from as far away as Belize and Tikal, as Muyil was probably an important ceremonial center for the goddess. To the left of El Castillo stands the double level **Templo del Sacerdote** (Temple of the Priest). Archeologists believe that the first level housed priests who conducted religious rituals in the small temple directly above.

A **sacbé** (white-stone path), of which traces still remain, linked **Muyil** and **Cobá**★★, covering a distance of more than 50km/31mi.

El Castillo, Muyil

Climbing the pyramid, Grupo Coba

©Canhi Franck/Dreamstime.com

COBÁ★★

47km/29mi west of Tulum; this archeological site can also be reached from Valladolid (59km/36.6mi) via Carr. 180 east. Open daily 8am–6pm. $4. The Nohoch Mul Group, Conjunto Pinturas and Macanxoc Group can be seen in about 2.5hrs.

Once the northeast Yucatán peninsula's largest city, Cobá in its heyday was home to 50,000–100,000 people. The city flourished in the Middle to Late Classic period, probably through partnership with Tikal (in Guatemala), while its later decline has been attributed to war with Chichén Itzá.

Nestled beside Cobá lake and surrounded by thick jungle vegetation, the surviving ceremonial complex's Mayan name means *"water ruffled by the wind,"* and in many ways it is the lakes, forest, birds, monkeys and other flora and fauna that make a visit to this monumental site so captivating. Only a few of Cobá's estimated 6,000 structures are restored or uncovered, but its vastness *(70sq km/27sq mi; bicycles are available for hire at the entrance, as are guides)* can give a sense of real solitude. The principal architectural complexes of the site are near the Cobá and Macanxoc lakes. Cobá's structures are connected by **sacbéob** (network of *sacbés* or white stone roads), which also link the city with other groups of buildings and pre-Hispanic settlements like **Yaxuná**, 100km/62mi away. The religious center is divided into four groups of structures: Cobá, Pinturas, Nohoch Mul and Macanxoc. These groups are dispersed throughout the thick jungle, but linked by shady trails, from 200m/656ft, to 2km/1.2mi long. Of the 43 structures that comprise the **Grupo Cobá**, the most important is the **Templo de la Iglesia**, 'Temple of the Church', second in height only to Nohoch Mul (there is a fantastic view of lake Macanxoc from the top, but climbing is forbidden). Built in the center of a plaza, the temple features a stela where offerings of candles and flowers are left by present-day Mayan peasants who claim that this stone statue represents the Virgin called "Colebí." The pyramid consists of nine sections with rounded corners 24m/78ft

Ball Court, Grupo Cobá

©Ken Thomas/ Wikimedia Commons

tall. The Cobá Group also has a **ball court**, and a large residential palace.

Grupo Nohoch Mul (*2km/1.2mi from the Cobá Group*) translates as "Large Hillock", testament to the pyramid's setting on a hillock, which sends it 42m/138ft into the sky, making it the tallest Mayan structure on the Yucatán peninsula (you may climb this structure). Nohoch Mul consists of seven round-cornered tiers with two staircases. The main staircase leads to a temple decorated with eastern coastal elements—niches and images of the Diving God. Approximately 100m/109yd ahead stands an enormous stela from the 8C AD that depicts a richly dressed Mayan ruler, with a scepter, flanked by diminutive warriors who appear kneeling and tied down.

Cobá's links with southerly city states like Tikal influenced the **Cobá style**, which flourished from the Early Classic (AD 300–600) to the Terminal Classic period (AD 900–1000): this demonstrates clear Petén similarities, with less embellishments than at Chichén Itzá, obvious today in the Cobá Group and Nohoch Mul.

RUTA RÍO BEC★★

With the exception of Calakmul, the Río Bec sites lie close to Carr. 186; they are listed here east–west (from the west, Río Bec is 290km/180mi from Campeche via Escárcega). All sites open daily 8am–5pm. Campeche: 981-811-9229; Chetumal: 983-835-0860.

The **Río Bec** subregion lies less than 100km/62mi from the Guate-

Mayan Ball Courts

Found in all but the smallest of Mayan cities, ballcourts were considered to be gateways to the underworld. Played using hips, shoulders and elbows, points were scored for goals and opposition errors. Ballcourt panels at Chichén Itzá indicate that in the Classic period sacrifice/beheading of players was a culminating event. It remains uncertain whether this was a punishment, a mechanism for dispatching enemies, or a fast-track to 'enlightenment' for team captains. The game may have been used as a proxy for warfare and settling disputes. Severed heads are featured in much Late Classic ballgame art and in the Post-Classic Mayan narrative **Popol Vuh**. Some speculate that heads and skulls were used as balls.

malan border and includes more than 50 archeological sites. Its cities, such as **Becán★★**, **Chicanná★**, **Xpuhil★**, and **Calakmul★★**, exercised control over extensive cultural subregions in modern Quintana Roo and southern Campeche, still distinguishable by their location and architectural styles. Calakmul (at the heart of the **Biósfera de Calakmul★**) fought against **Tikal** (in modern Guatemala) for leadership in this region during the Late Classic period. All of these cultures reached their peak between AD 500 and 800. Considered a link between the Petén (Guatemala) and Chenes (Northern Campeche) styles, Río Bec's distinctive features are tall, steep towers with false stairways flanking the principal buildings. Other characteristics are structures built on broad platforms, large constructions with rounded corners, fretwork motifs and large masks of the god **Itzamná**, also called the "Earth Monster," represented by reptiles with open jaws. The rain forest is prolific here despite the heat and lack of water; it successfully hid the Río Bec's archeological treasures for over 1,200 years.

Dzibanché & Kinichná★

68km/43mi west of Chetumal on Carr. 186; follow signs for 24km/14.9mi north to Dzibanché/Kinichná fork in the road: The sites are respectively 1.5km/1mi and 3km/2mi further. Open daily 8am–5pm. $3-4.

Surrounded by forest, Dzibanché and Kinichná were sister cities and united formed one of the greatest regional powers in southern

Quintana Roo during the Mayan Classic period (AD 100–1000). Their largely un-excavated sites are protected by forested hillocks populated by flocks of parrots and other birds.

Notably at **Dzibanché**, the hieroglyphics carved on the lintels of **Edificio 6** (Building 6) give the site its name, which means "writing on wood." An original lintel with a calendar inscription of AD 733 adorns the opening in the southern wall of the upper temple. South of Edificio 6 lie two plazas. The one to the east is surrounded by long **palaces** and by **Edificio 2**, the tallest building on the site. Both are considered funeral monuments due to their tombs with rich offerings. The inhabitants of Dzibanché settled a wide area and constructed sites for worshipping their gods and rulers. **Kinichná**, an elevated architectural complex (*2km/1.2mi from Dzibanché*) of three-tiered elements where temples of ceremonial and funerary character were built, may have been one of these.

On the top tier is a tomb of two rulers with some of the most refined jade artifacts ever discovered in the region. Remains of large masks flank the steps.

©Yucatán Today

Dzibanché

Mayan Mask, Kohunlich

Kohunlich★★

1km/.6mi west from the turning for Dzibanché; take the left turn, and continue 9km/5.6mi. $4–5.

Named by archeologists "the hillock of corozo palms" after the tall trees that proliferate here, Kohunlich was a ceremonial center with ample ties to the Petén region of Guatemala, displaying architectural features typical of the region in the remains of the **acrópolis**' tall towers.

At the rear of the site stands the main building, discovered by a Mayan hunter in the 1960s. The five **masks★★** that adorn the facade are impressively large (1.5m/5ft tall), with fine stucco decoration still marked with original red pigment. Representing Kinich Ahau, (the "Sun-face," one of the Maya's most important deities), the masks' eyes are inscribed with a hieroglyph representing the symbol *Kin*, which signifies the sun, day and time. A few steps from the Temple of the Masks, toward the right, lies a **ball court** in excellent condition. Walk along the jungle-path to admire more partly-restored buildings that were used as living quarters. You finally reach the **Estructura de los 27 Escalones** (The 27 Step Structure). This was recently consolidated from the remains of a residential complex constructed between AD 600 and 1200. From the top there is a splendid **view** of the area.

Xpuhil★

116km/72mi west of Chetumal on Carr. 186. $3–4.

A trail leads through dense forest to **Estructura I★**, an 18m/59ft-tall building characterized by its three towers—atypical in Río Bec architecture—and their dangerous verticality. The central tower,

Estructura I, Xpuhil

Estructura VIII, Becán

©Varga Tamás/Wikimedia Commons

comprised of 11 sections, is the best preserved of all the structures and, like its companions, was once crowned by a simulated temple. It was also once flanked by a 6m/19.6ft-wide staircase with three large fantastic masks (still partly visible). Vestiges of stucco ornamentation representing Chaac, the rain god, are preserved on the lower sidewalls. Toward the left side of the south tower, a steep, narrow staircase leads to an opening at the top. *Xpuhil*, meaning "cat's tail," is the name of a local herb. The nearby village of Xpuhil has lodgings for those looking to explore the area (*see Must Stay*).

Becán★★

6km/3.7mi west of Xpuhil turn to Becán, 500m/547yd from the highway. $3–4.

This once very large city can be seen from the highway. Becán's main buildings were protected by a moat 5m/16.4ft deep and 16m/52.5ft wide that ran 1.9km/1.2mi around the city. Boasting seven entrances, each with a bridge, Becán's design testifies to the constant invasions of the Classic period. Becán, which means "gully" or "water canyon," was the political, economic and religious capital of the province now called Río Bec. This archeological site was discovered in 1934 by two researchers from the Carnegie Institute. The first excavations took place between 1969 and 1971, while most of the restoration work was completed between 1991 and 2004.

In **Plaza A** lies a circular altar associated with Kukulcán, the wind god. To the south stands **Estructura I**, featuring 15m/49ft-high towers, and on whose upper level were found openings that may have allowed for astronomical observations.

To the northeast, the **vaulted passageway★** served as a street in ancient Becán and was covered by a Mayan arch along its length of nearly 60m/65.6yd. This passageway leads to **Plaza B**, bordered to the west by the monumental **Estructura VIII**, which supports two large towers at its north and south ends; eight tall (8m/26ft high) dark chambers here may have been used for religious ceremonies.

MAYAN CITIES

To the north is **Estructura IX**, the site's tallest building (32m/105ft). To the west is **Estructura X**. In 2001, archeologists excavated a stunning stucco mask here, which can be seen through a window. Behind this building is the **Juego de Pelota** (ball court).

Chicanná★

From Becán return to Carr. 186, continue west 2km/1.3mi and turn left onto the dirt road continuing for 500m/547yd. $3–4.

Chicanná's beginnings date back to the Late Pre-Classic period (300 BC–AD 250), but it flourished around AD 850. A hunter discovered the site in 1966. Archeologists named the site the 'House of the Serpent's Mouth' (*Chicanná* in Mayan) because of the **facade★★** of Estructura II, one of the most complete and best-preserved images of the god Itzamná. The door bay simulates the open jaws of a serpent, the fangs of which descend menacingly from the lintel. The facade symbolizes the entrance into the bowels of this powerful deity, creator of all things

according to Mayan mythology. Above can be seen the remains of crestings that held images for worship. Painted hieroglyphics adorn the sides of the portal.

Calakmul★★

From Xpuhil go west on Carr. 186. After 50km/31.2mi turn left at the sign for Calakmul and pass for 60km/37.5mi through the Biósfera de Calakmul★. $3–4 (archeological site), $2 (reserve).

Calakmul, deep inside the jungle of southern Campeche, has more than 6,000 structures, the majority of which are still well hidden. Calakmul once administered a large domain marked by the extensive distribution of the city's snake head emblem. **Tikal** and Calakmul were active competitors for resources in the region, waging almost constant war in the Terminal Classic period. Tikal ultimately overcame Calakmul, which descended into obscurity from the 11C onward. This ancient Mayan city was discovered in 1931 but then forgotten, until exploration started again in the 1990s.

Facade of Estructura II, Chicanná

Estructura II, Calakmul

The name comes from the Mayan words "*Ca*" (two) "*Lak*" (nearby), and "*Mul*" (mound) meaning 'the city of two adjacent mounds'. Those mounds are impressive pyramids, which rise high above the jungle canopy. The highest is **Estructura I** (53m/177ft). A well-maintained path leads to the most important structures and complexes including the **Gran Acrópolis** and the **Gran Plaza**.

MUSEUMS

Isla Cozumel Museums

San Miguel★, the capital of **Isla Cozumel★★**, is home to the **Museo de la Isla★** (*San Miguel, corner of Av. Rafael E. Melgar and Av. 6 norte; open daily 9am–5pm; $3; 987-872-0914*). The first floor is dedicated to Cozumel's natural history and features a display on reefs, while the second floor recounts the history of the island from the ancient Mayan era, including objects and artifacts from **San Gervasio★**. The museum also showcases the Spanish conquest and the history of Cozumel during the 19C and 20C.

Also on Cozumel, .5mi from San Miguel, is **Discover Mexico** (*Km5.5, Carr. Costera Sur, Zona Hotelera Sur, 987-857-2820, www. discovermexico.org*), a combination indoor exhibition space, and outdoor museum where multilingual guides lead visitors around large-scale models of Mexico's most important cities and archeological sites.

Chetumal Museum

The capital of Quintana Roo, with a population of 136,000, Chetumal 's city center is home to the **Museo de la Cultura Maya★** (*Av. Héroes and Mahatma Gandhi, in front of the market; open Tue–Thu & Sun 9am–7pm, Fri & Sat 9am–8pm; $5. 983-832-6838*), a modern museum presenting an overview of pre-Hispanic Mayan civilization—earthly life, the underworld and the heavenly vault, joined by the image of the sacred silk-cotton tree. Replicas of important discoveries, large models and visitor-friendly interactive screens help illustrate the physical, daily and architectural features as well as the scientific advances of the ancient Maya.

MAYAN CITIES

OUTDOOR ACTIVITIES

If you can pry yourself away from the beach, there is so much more to do in Cozumel and the South. The beautiful natural environment sets the stage for some eclectic golf courses, as well as jungle tours on horseback, forest zip-lining, ATV tours and much more.

GOLF

On the northwest point of **Isla Cozumel★★**, 15 minutes from the international pier and 10 minutes from Cozumel Airport is the **Cozumel Country Club** (*Carr. Costera Norte, Km6.5, Interior Casa Club Cozumel; 987-872-9570; www. cozumelcountryclub.com.mx*). The Jack Nicklaus designed course (par 72, 6,734 yard) is Cozumel's first, and has over 60 bunkers and water hazards over 18 holes, winding through jungle and mangroves. Along the course you may see native wildlife from iguanas to wild pigs and even the odd crocodile. It took five years to sculpt the limestone, coral and saltwater marshes to preserve the environmental integrity. There's a clubhouse, shops and snack bar. Back on the mainland at **Playa del Carmen★★**, the **Playacar Golf Club** (*shuttles available, Paseo Xaman-ha s/n, M 26 Fraccionamiento Playacar, 984-873-4990; www.*

palaceresorts.com), is a championship course (par 72, 7,144 yards) and probably the most challenging in the region. Designed by Robert Von Hagge, the course is carved out of dense jungle a few hundred yards from the ocean. The Mayan-style clubhouse and spa keeps partners happy, while the golf carts come equipped with GPS so you can find your way back, as well as electronic leaderboards and food and beverage ordering, should you not wish to return.

Just north of Playa del Carmen, **El Camaléon** (*Carr. 307 Km298; 984-206-3000; www.maya koba.com; www.fairmont.com*) borders the plush AAA Five Diamond Fairmont **Mayakoba** resort (*see Resorts*), a 240-acre complex surrounded by canals, shoreline and mangrove forests. Greg Norman's first Mexican course features 18 challenging holes through a Caribbean park-ride of jungle,

El Camaléon Golf Course

©Courtesy of OHL, El Camaléon, Mayakoba, Mexico

swamp, ocean and mangroves. In fact, **El Camaléon** has become so popular with golf-aficionados, that it was the first dip south of the border for the PGA.

Also in the Playa area, the **Mayan Palace Riviera Golf Club** (*Carr. 307 Km48; 984-206-4002; www. grupomayangolf.com; www.grupo mayan.com*) has a Jack Nicklaus designed, 18 hole par 54, 2,923 yard course. The greens were cut out of the jungle, and fees include golf cart, drinks and food.

Further south at **Puerto Aventuras** (*Carr.Chetumal Km269.5, Pto. Juarez/Pto. Aventuras; www.puerto aventuras.com*) is a 9-hole par 36, 3,236 yard course designed by Thomas Leeman and surrounded by tropical foliage.

TOURS AND ACTIVITIES

Also see Nature and Cenotes.

On Isla Cozumel a number of organizations provide horseback rides, ATV tours and jungle treks.

Explora Tours, (*987-869-0080; www.exploratours.com*) runs a bike and snorkel beach trek, clear kayak trips, dune buggy and beach snorkeling, reef snorkeling, a folklore show and shopping trip, and a jeep trip. During the latter excursion, you drive a four-person jeep to the eastern island and head north (*see Beaches*) for 20 minutes of off-roading, before returning to Pelicanos Beach for a Mexican lunch and some off-shore snorkeling with experienced guides.

You might also try **Cozumel Tours**, (*322-222-4935, Mx Toll-free 1-800-822-4577, US/Can Toll-free 866-728-1438; www.cozumel-tours. com*) who can arrange just about anything you want to do from

Ancient Mayan road in Cozumel

©DeannaBean/iStockphoto.com

horseback riding to ATV tours and jungle hikes.

Mr. Sancho's Beach Club (*south of downtown San Miguel at Km15 on the main road; 998-112-1933; www.mrsanchos.com*) between the Reef Club and the Allegro Resort also organizes horseback riding and ATV tours. A one hour ride is $41; $49.50 includes use of beach club and a buffet lunch.

For a treetop view of Cozumel, try **Fly High Adventures** (*7.2km/ 4.5mi/10min south of San Miguel on the main road; 987-872-0844*) where ziplines take you over a small ecopark.

Back on the mainland the **Puerto Morelos★** area has a number of jungle and horse-riding tours popular with visitors daytripping from **Cancún★★** (*see Cancún*). Further south in the Playa del Carmen area, just 10 minutes north of town, the **Playa Maroma Paradise** (*www.maromaparadise.com*) development has a 2.5hr tour of mangroves, beach and sea. Patrons, divided into three groups by ability level, ride through the jungle for 80 minutes, then after resting, they can swim in the water with the horse for about 25 minutes.

WATERSPORTS

The Caribbean coast's beaches (*see Beaches*) and resorts (*see Must Stay*) have an endless supply of activities like hobie cat sailing and parasailing, while coastal mangroves and inlets in places like **Sian-Ka'an★★** (*see Nature and Cenotes*) are perfect for exploring in a canoe or kayak. However, it should come as no surprise that the denizens of the deep are the real draw of the waters, from exciting deep-sea and flats fishing, to **swimming with dolphins**.

For scuba and snorkeling see Meso-American Reef.

SPORTFISHING

One of the best things about **Cozumel fishing** is that it's only a few minutes from shore, so you really maximize your time casting or trolling. The fishing is excellent all year long, with a few species not available for a few months at different seasons. There's deep sea fishing for large billfish like marlin and tuna, and exciting fly fishing for bonefish, snook, permit, and others. Trips up to the Cancún flats, or further south to fishing centers like **Puerto Aventuras** or **Sian-Ka'an★★** have a stunning variety for deep-sea, estuary and flats fishing. The options listed here are a selection from the region.

Isla Cozumel★★

Since 1975 Carlos Vega has been running fishing trips in the Cozumel area at **Aquarius Grand Slam Fishing** (*3 South Street #2 betw Av. Rafael E. Melgar and 5a Av.; 987-869-1096, 987-872-1165, www.aquariusflatsfishing.com*), with catches including bill fish, tarpon, permit and the elusive bonefish. Carlos runs trips out to the fishing flats north of Cancún at Isla Blanca (best Dec–Feb), as well as the better bonefishing flats around Cozumel (catch huge permit Mar–Dec), while his deep-sea charters take you out for bigger game.

If deep-sea fishing is your bag, try **Cozumel Fishing Center**, (*Carr. Costera Sur Km5, Interior Marina Caleta; 9am–9pm; 1-800-605-9490; www.cozumelfishingcenter.com*) for marlin, sailfish, mahi mahi, shark, snapper, wahoo, barracuda, and amberjack. Boats leave from Marina Caleta.

Boats from **Cozumel Charters** (*987-869-8560, US & CAN Toll-free 1-866-645-8977; www.fishingcozumel.net*) leave from Marinas Caleta and Puerto Abrigo and hotel piers (plus Puerto Aventuras on the mainland).

Puerto Aventuras

In **Puerto Aventuras** there are plenty of options for fishing. **Tequila Sunrise Adventures** (*www.chartermexico.com*) has year-round charters and fishing for billfish, marlin, sailfish, tuna, wahoo as well as sports fish species.

Dolphins entertaining at Puerto Aventuras

©Steve Hodder/BigStockPhoto.com

With **Capt. Rick's Adventures**, (984-873-5195, 984-873-5387; www. captricksfishing.com) you will troll for sailfish, marlin, wahoo and dorado right outside the Puerto Aventuras marina, with year-round sport fishing charters and English-speaking captains.

Reserva de la Biósfera de Sian-Ka'an★★

Out on the **Punta Allen** Peninsula in Sian-Ka'an Biosphere, **Boca Paila Fishing Lodge**, (984-155-0012, Toll-free US 800-245-1950; www.bocapailamexico.com) sits on a combination of fresh and brackish estuaries with a complex shallow-water reef system. The environment provides superb bonefishing, a large permit population, tarpon, snook, barracuda, jack crevalle and cubera snapper. Private fishing charters are available. Choose from deep sea fishing (half or whole day), fly fishing, or fishing and snorkeling combo (full day).

©Boca Paila Fishing Lodge
Catching permit at Boca Paila

©World Pictures/Photoshot
Reserva de la Biósfera de Sian-Ka'an

Bahía de Chetumal
The small fishing village of **Xcalak** is a haven for flyfishing enthusiasts; Chetumal Bay flats provide large numbers of bonefish and permit. Try Victor Castro's fishing tours (US call: 011-52-983-839-1444; www.xcalak-flyfishing.com).

DOLPHIN SWIM
Dolphin swim programs are popping up everywhere on the Caribbean coast, with several operations vying for your pesos. The largest organization is **Dolphin Discovery**, which has various sites in the region.

Cozumel has two dolphin programs, the original one at Chankanaab National Park, run by Dolphin Discovery, and a new one near downtown, run by Dolphinaris. **Chankanaab National Park★★** (see Introduction/ Nature and Cenotes; 987-872-0914; www.cozumelparks.com) has an excellent program and the design of the facility makes it almost feel as though you are out on the reef. Just south of downtown, **Dolphinaris** (Km1.5 Zona Hotelera Sur, entre Calle 17 y 19; www.dolphinaris.com) is a new development that seeks to give the dolphins a semi-natural environment, with 14,000sq ft of natural ocean coves. On the **Riviera Maya★★★** you can swim with dolphins with **Delphinus** (998-206-3304; www.delphinusworld.com) at **Xel-Há★★** (Km24) and **Xcaret★★★** (Km282), as well as at a new facility opening at Uvero on the **Costa Maya★★** not far from Mahahual.

WATERSPORTS

SAILING AND CRUISING

The stunning coastline of the Caribbean coast is an adventure playground for the budding sailor, or simply for a passenger looking for a quiet perch to sip a cold beer and trail a foot in the turquoise waters.

Catamaran trip

©Tony Moore/BigStockPhoto.com

BOAT TOURS

If you don't feel like scuba diving in Cozumel, why not become a submariner aboard the **Atlantis Submarine** (*Carr. a Chankanaab Km4; $84 adult/$45 12 and under; 987-872-5671, 987-872-435; www.atlantisadventures.com*). The 40-minute trip on a real submarine sees you dive to 30m to discover myriad fish and large coral heads just like a scuba diver. A number of local operators in the region run **glass-bottom boat** tours of the various reefs, **speedboat** tours and **catamaran** trips where the drinks flow freely. You can book in advance online, or locally. The marinas listed under 'Sailing' are home to various pleasure boat and charter companies.

SAILING

On Cozumel at **Puerto Abrigo Marina**, **Cozumel Sailing** (*Puerto Abrigo, the north marina on the island. 987-869-2312; www.cozumel sailing.com*) provide a variety of options, from daytrips aboard their 35ft Tri-maran "Tucan", to fishing trips and private sailing charters. Experienced sailors can hire the 22ft "Jenna Lynn" sloop (takes up to 6 people) as a bareboat rental. Instructions and crew are also available. You can even learn to sail with an instructor for $12.50 per hour. Rental rates start at $100 for two hours, additional hours are $25.00. The day rate special is $200. 30 miles south of Cancún in **Puerto Morelos★**, is **Marina El Cid Cancún** (*Blvd. El Cid Unidad 15, 77580 Puerto Morelos; 998-871-0184; www.elcid.com*), which accommodates 300 vessels ranging from 25–120ft. Facilities include a sportfishing fleet, dive shop, snorkeling, sailing, day cruises and ecological tours. Shuttles run to Cancún and Playa del Carmen daily. A taxi service is available 24 hours a day, just a few minutes from the Harbor Master's office.

Further south on the Riviera Maya, **Puerto Aventuras** (*Km269.5 Carr. 307; Harbour Master Gerardo Segrove Serrano; 984-873-5108; www.puertoaventuras.com.mx*) has a deep draught, full service marina, including room service! The daily rate is $8 for boats under 30ft, and between $1.15 and $1.68 per foot over that. Small sailboats cost $17 a day in low season, or $25 in high season. Longer term rates are available, as are day sailing trips and sailboat charters.

CRUISING

Cozumel★★ is one of the top cruise port destinations in the Caribbean, with over 50 ships calling here regularly and three **cruise ship piers**. The Punta Langosta Pier is just a five-minute walk to downtown, the SSA International Pier just offshore from the **Park Royal Hotel** (3km/2mi/5min drive out of town), while the Puerta Maya Pier is a few

Marina Cozumel

Ever forward-looking, Cozumel is developing "**Marina Cozumel**" adjacent to the Presidente Inter-Continental Resort and Spa, to house up to 332 vessels, 60ft or less and provide a laundry list of services. Included in the plan are luxury residential units, condos, hotel accommodations, and boutiques and shops.

minutes past the International. There are plenty of taxis at each pier, the quickest and easiest and way to get downtown. The hitlist for cruisers short on time should include: scuba diving and snorkeling, a visit to **Chankanaab National Park★★**, **Faro Celarain Eco Park★★**, an inland jungle tour, **San Gervasio★**, a cenote trip and a walk around **San Miguel★**. On the **Costa Maya★★**, the cruise ship dock near the once sleepy fishing village of **Mahahual** receives up to three cruise ships a day.

©Ramunas Bruzas/BigStockPhoto.com

Cruise ship arriving at Cozumel

SAILING & CRUISING

91

SHOPPING

The best shopping on this stretch of coast is found on Isla Cozumel and at Playa del Carmen, but there are plenty of other places for spending your hard-earned dollars.

BEST BUYS

The best buys are on Mexican liquors like **tequila**, **Kahlua**, and a specialty liqueur called **Xtaben-tum**. Pronounced '*Sh-ta-ben-tun*' (Mayan for "vines growing on stone"), this Mayan sweet liqueur is made exclusively in the Yucatán. Honey extracted from *Xtabentum* flowers (that only grow in the Yucatán) is distilled with anise & rum. The best souvenirs include **leather goods**, and local **arts and crafts** items (check the label to see where it was made). Mexican **silver jewelry** and knick knacks are excellent gifts, but check for the engraved .825 silver mark. Even so, if the price is much lower in one place than everywhere else, think twice. Don't forget to check the shops at the archeological sites and nature parks for unusual gifts.

TOURS

There are many people selling rugs, hammocks, and all sorts of souvenirs along the road and outside the entrance to the ruins.

If you go on a bus tour, the guide might stop at a "Lapis Factory", or "jewelry factory", etc., because the guide gets a commission on anything you buy there. The bus might also stop in front of a "preferred vendor". In general items will cost more here than elsewhere. When people get back on the bus and compare purchases, they find that one person paid double what another person paid for the same exact thing.

CORAL

As a general rule you should never buy coral. Reefs take millennia to develop and only a few years (or even months) to die, particularly when they are plundered for sale to tourists. When the reefs are gone (and they are being destroyed by tourism daily), so is one of the major reasons for coming here. In particular, you should never buy Black Coral. It is beautiful and locally grown, but endangered and illegal to bring into the US and other countries.

Silver jewelry on sale at Playa del Carmen

©longhorndwice/iStockphoto.com

Bargaining

You can bargain with almost everyone, even in the high-end shops if you are really interested in buying something, and if you're nice about it. Vendors expect it and the first asking price is always about two thirds more than they expect to get in the end. If you are in the market for an expensive item, do your research before you leave home.

It is also fairly easy to duplicate black coral and relatively difficult to tell the difference.

ISLA COZUMEL

Business hours: 9am–2pm, 5pm–10pm, but many shops are open all day.

Cozumel has three main shopping areas. The first, in **San Miguel**, is along the waterfront and all around the town square (the "Plaza del Sol"), and going back several blocks in all directions. Around the Plaza are pharmacies, dive shops, and just about everything else. The second shopping area is the town's **crafts market** behind the plaza, and the third is the **cruise ship terminals**, especially the mall at the Punta Langosta pier. Cozumel prices are generally a bit high, but everything costs more the closer you get to the port. Another shopping axiom: as soon as you buy something, you'll likely find it cheaper at the next shop! There's a big department store, **Chedraui**, at the southern end of town. A **Commercial Mexicano** megastore opened in 2008, and there are three smaller markets: **Cozumel Market** on Adolfo Rosado Salas between 20th and 25th, and **San Francisco**—one on Av. 65, the other on Av. 30 and Juarez.

RIVIERA MAYA

Outside of the "Big Three"—Cozumel, Cancún, and Playa del Carmen—look for interesting artisania in the small towns, and in the gift shops of archeological sites, museums, and natural attractions. The marina in **Puerto Aventuras** has some eclectic shops, while **Akumal** has unique shops for Mexican arts and crafts, jewelry, and textiles. Downtown **Tulum** had a face-lift not long ago, to keep pace with its transformation into the next Playa del Carmen, but it still has traditional shops.

Souvenir shop, Cozumel

©Tony Moore/BigStockPhoto.com

KIDS

The island of **Cozumel★★** and the **Riviera Maya★★★** are ideal for care-free family beach holidays with large hotels providing myriad services and carefully managed activities. Down on the **Costa Maya★★** you will find more peace and quiet, and tourism developments in the region create more services each year. All of this and you are staying in the heart of an adventureland of exotic ruins, mangroves, jungle and wild-life, with world-class snorkeling and diving. What's more, many facilities here excel at bringing the wilderness to kids, but in a safe environment.

The region's **beaches** (see Beaches), **reefs** (see Meso-American Reef) and **cenotes** (see Nature and Cenotes) provide so many options from **snorkeling** to **windsurfing** to **swimming with dolphins** (see Watersports), that it can be hard to leave the coastline at all. Isla Co-zumel and the Riviera Maya have plenty of **boating** opportunities like **glass-bottom boat** tours, transparent **kayaks** for exploring the seas under your own steam, and even a **submarine** adventure for budding Captain Nemos (see Sailing and Cruising).

If you are on Cozumel and you're short on time but want a taste of the region's Mayan sites, you must head over to **San Gervasio★**. If you have longer, out on the Riviera Maya you can adventure to mysterious **Cobá★★** shrouded in deep forest, beautiful **Tulum★★** perched overlooking a turquoise sea (see Mayan Cities), or mighty **Chichén Itzá★★★** in the Yucatán (see Yucatán and West), as well as a host of other captivating ruins. True Indiana Jones wannabes must make the journey to the **Río Bec★★** (see Mayan Cities) and its mammoth ruins, many still undiscovered under the jungle of the land of the jaguar.

The cool river that carves through limestone at **Xcaret★★★** (see Nature and Cenotes), is ideal for kids, with extensive facilities for children in a managed eco-park environment. **Xel-Há★★** has equally suitable facilities and is a great place to bring children.

Jungle adventurers will appreciate Cozumel's zip-line **treetop tours**. For weary explorers, a bite for lunch and a warm sea for a dip make a perfect end to **horseback rides** and treks along the jungle floor. For a real slice of nature, from seeing crocodiles and exotic birds, to mon-keys and swarms of brightly colored butterflies, you must venture to **Faro Celerain Ecopark★★**, **Sian-Ka'an★★** or **Calakmul★** Biospheres (see Nature and Cenotes). With the right tour the latter two are fantastic experiences for older children (with the energy for it). Alternatively there are several ecoprojects operating sustainable tourism within the vicin-ity of the biosphere reserves, so you can stay locally and take short trips without ruffling feathers.

Snorkeling in Cozumel waters

© Cozumel Promotion Board

RELAX

From **Cozumel★★** to **Tulum★★** there are innumerable spas, many providing treatments using ancient Mayan techniques of purifying, cleansing, rebuilding, rejuvenating, relaxing, and beautifying body and mind.

COZUMEL

 Mandara Spa – *In the Presidente InterContinental Resort & Spa (see Resorts).* Opened March 2007, this unique spa, finished in warm wood, is circular to promote positive energy. It has the latest equipment, large treatment rooms, and attentive staff. In addition to traditional European and Asian massage, choose from exotic treatments inspired by ancient Mayan rituals. On the grounds there is also a Temazcal sweat lodge.

Islander Spa – *In the Wyndham Cozumel Resort & Spa (see Resorts).* The largest spa facility in Cozumel (8,000 sq ft.), the Islander Spa was created to provide a relaxing environment that contributes to the renewal process. The trained staff is certified in diverse techniques and therapies for both individual and couple treatments.

Acqua Spa – *Carr. Costera Sur Km2.4, 987-872-7192, www.acquaspa.com.mx.* A premier day spa, 5min south of town with extensive services, including seven types of massage, body wraps, facials, and other techniques such as Endermologie to help relax and revitalize mind and body.

PUERTO MORELOS

Ceiba del Mar – *Puerto Morelos, 998-872-8060. www.ceibadelmar.com.*

Paradisus Riviera Cancún – *1-866-436-3542. www.paradisus-riviera-cancun.com.*

Paraiso de la Bonita – *998-872-8300. www.paraisodelabonita.com.*

PLAYA DEL CARMEN

Auriga spa – *Capella Bahía Maroma. 984-803-4571. www.capellalivingmaroma.com.*

El Spa – *Iberostar. US Toll-free: 1-888-923-2722. www.iberostar.com.*

Hacienda Trés Ríos – *998-891-5263. www.haciendatresrios.com.*

Mandarin Oriental Riviera Maya – *984 877 3888. www.mandarinoriental.com.*

Maroma Resort & Spa – *998-872-8200. www.maromahotel.com.*

Reef Playacar – *1-800-714-0220. www.thereefplayacar.com.*

Sense Spa – *984-875-8000. www.rosewoodmayakoba.com.*

Spa Itzá – *984-803-2588. http://spaitza.com.*

The Tides – *984-877-3000. www.tidesrivieramaya.com.*

The Village Esthetic Spa – *984-803-4529. www.villageestheticspa.com.*

Willow Stream Spa – *Fairmont Mayakoba. 984-206-3000. www.fairmont.com.*

XCARET

Xcaret – *1-800-2-XCARET. www.xcaret.com.*

XEL-HÁ

Esencia – *984-873-4835. www.hotelesencia.com.*

Xel-Há – *998-884-7165. www.xelha.com.*

TULUM

Aventura Spa Palace – *984-875-1100. www.palaceresorts.com.*

EcoTulum Resorts & Spa – *888-898-9922, www.maya-spa.com.*

YUCATÁN AND WEST

The geography of the Yucatán is considered by many to be the cause of its exceptional cultural activity, past and present. It is also what makes it so magical. Long stretches of low flat lands, verdant green, lie over the porous limestone plain whose underwater currents dot the surface in blue-water cenotes. Though human civilization has thrived here for millennia, the expanse of foliage that lies between man's comings and goings hides a land where the jaguar is still king.

MUST SEE YUCATÁN & WEST

Casa del Adivino (Pyramid of the Magician), Uxmal

©Angelika/iStockphoto.com

WHERE TO GO

The states of Yucatán and Campeche are replete with possible day trips in all directions and for all tastes and interests. Base yourself in the colonial cities of **Campeche★**, **Mérida★★** and **Valladolid★★** (*see Colonial Cities*) to enjoy the charm of cobblestone streets and Spanish architecture as you rest between jaunts to neighboring pre-Hispanic cities, haciendas, convents, cenotes, beaches or natural reserves.

Or, you can well base yourself within a hacienda, above a cenote, or alongside a pre-Hispanic city to enjoy the quiet of a dark night while you venture to colonial cities by day for their museums and movement.

For more information on regional touring opportunities, check with Mérida-based **EcoTurismo** Yucatán (*www.ecoyuc.com*), Mayan Heritage (*mayanheritage.com. mx*), and Mayan Ecotours (*www. mayanecotours.com*).

UXMAL AREA

Uxmal★★★, declared a World Heritage Site in 1996, is the magnificent gateway to what is known today as the **Ruta Puuc★**. Though its name means "three times built", little is known about the history of the city, and its most impressive **pyramid** has evidence of being built five times, not three. Thought to have been regional capital of the Puuc cities, Uxmal represents the quintessence of the Puuc Architectural style, typical of the Late Classic period from AD600–900. **Exploring the Area** – After exploring the site, continue east on

Carr. 261 to reach **Kabáh**. **Sayil**★ lies further south (turn left off 261), followed by **Xlapak**, **Labná**★ and the **Grutas de Loltún**★★. You can also take the **Ruta Puuc Day Bus** (*Autotransportes del Sur, ATS, www. ticketbus.com.mx*) for $13, which leaves daily at 8am from the Terminal de Segunda Clase on Calle 69 between 68 and 70.

The tour will afford you just enough time to form a general idea of each site; some 2 hours at **Uxmal**★★★ and half an hour each at the other sites. You can also stay behind in Uxmal for the sound and light show, which involves an overnight stay.

See Nature and Cenotes; Mayan Cities; Must Stay; Shopping.

CAMPECHE AREA

The walled city of **Campeche**★, built on the Mayan site called Ah Kin Pech or "place of the sun tick", may be one of Mexico's best kept secrets. Indeed, secrecy is as entrenched in this seaside colonial gem as the gold in a pirate's hidden cave. Though Spaniards first arrived here in 1517, two years before Hernán Cortes arrived at Tenochtitlán, they were unable to

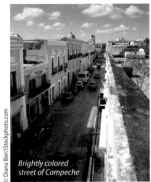

© Diana Bier/iStockphoto.com

Brightly colored street of Campeche

conquer the Mayan warriors they met until 1540, when the victorious Francisco de Montejo officially founded the "Villa de San Francisco de Campeche."

Exploring the Area – From Campeche explore ancient cities built by the Chenes and Itzaes who eventually arrived at **Chichén Itzá**★★★. Journey into the thick jungle wall to help uncover the mysteries found in the **Río Bec**★★ sites (*see Cozumel & South*), only recently coming to light. Bask in the sun with a gentle gulf breeze at one of the area's long quiet **beaches**, where the white sand is

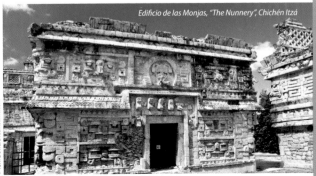

Edificio de las Monjas, "The Nunnery", Chichén Itzá

© Tom Dowd/Dreamstime.com

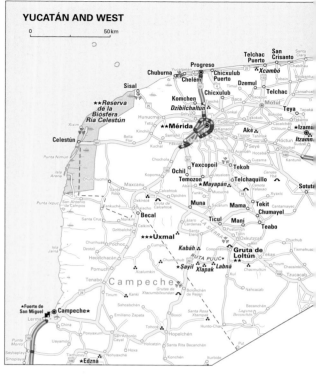

YUCATÁN AND WEST

0 ——— 50km

actually finely broken seashells, or relax in a hacienda-spa.
See Beaches; Colonial Cities; Mayan Cities, Shopping; Kids; Must Relax.

CELESTÚN AREA

The **Reserva de la Biósfera de Ría Celestún★★**, which lies between Yucatán and Campeche, is among the most important Gulf sites for wintering birds on the central migratory flyway, and is home to more than 320 winged species. Here you can see Mother Nature's spectacular hues between March and August when pink flamingos leave their nests and come

in droves to feed on the area's rich phyto- and zoo-planktons.
Exploring the Area – On your way to or from Celestún you can turn off the highway at Huncuma and head west to **Sisal**, yesterday's hopping port and today's quiet beach retreat. You can also head southeast to **Uxmal★★★**, or south to **Campeche★**.
See Nature and Cenotes; Outdoor Activities; Kids; Must Relax.

MÉRIDA AREA

"The White City" was built by Francisco de Montejo and his cohort on the Mayan center of T'ho, a

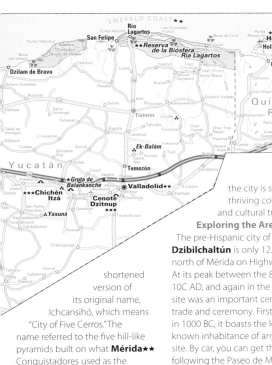

shortened version of its original name, Ichcansihó, which means "City of Five Cerros." The name referred to the five hill-like pyramids built on what **Mérida★★** Conquistadores used as the foundations of their Plaza Mayor. Indeed, the very stones that made up these buildings were used in the Spaniards' constructions. Today the city is still a thriving colonial and cultural treasure.

Exploring the Area – The pre-Hispanic city of **Dzibilchaltún** is only 12.5 miles north of Mérida on Highway 261. At its peak between the 8C and 10C AD, and again in the 13C, this site was an important center of trade and ceremony. First settled in 1000 BC, it boasts the longest known inhabitance of any Mayan site. By car, you can get there by following the Paseo de Montejo past colonias and shopping centers and into the countryside. At 15km/9.3mi turn right and continue another 5km/3.1mi to the site.

Templo de las siete muñecas (Temple of the Seven Dolls), Dzibilchaltún

©World Pictures/Photoshot

The port at **Progreso**, only recently making a name for itself on tourist maps, is another 8mi north by the main highway, 26. You can also take a bus from the Terminal on Calle 62 between 65 and 67. From Progreso, getting around the different **seaside towns** that dot the coast is easily maneuvered with local combis available in town centers. From here you can explore the small ruins at **Xcambo**, or make your way northeast toward the Nature Reserve **Dzilam de Bravo**.
See Beaches, Nature and Cenotes; Colonial Cities; Mayan Cities, Outdoor Activities; Sailing and Cruising; Shopping; Kids; Must Relax.

Cenote Ik-Kil

©Joseph Calev/iStockphoto.com

VALLADOLID AREA

Some 42km/26mi east of **Chichén Itzá★★★** lies lovely colonial **Valladolid★★**. Officially named "the honey capital of the world", this second most important city in Yucatán state was founded in 1543 on the ancient city of Zací by Francisco de Montejo el Mozo. Today a **cenote** of the same name can be easily reached on foot from the city's main square. Navigate the center on foot; it is a fabulous

city to get lost in for a while. You can also rent a bike at Albergues La Candelaria on Calle 35 between 42 and 44 (*985-856-2267*) to visit nearby cenotes and ruins.
Exploring the Area – The incomparable pre-Hispanic city and ceremonial center of **Chichén Itzá**, "the city on the edge of the water sorcerer's well", was inhabited as early as 300 BC by agricultural communities, and was regional capital in the Late and Post Classic period from AD750–1200. Named a World Heritage Site in 1988, the city is pristinely kept, such that it

Valladolid's main square at night

©Sybille Yates/Dreamstime.com

feels like new, despite the 1500 years it has seen come and go. A stay at Valldaolid or Chichén Itzá will give you to explore many of the area's sites of interest, such as the cenote **Ik-Kil★★**, the **Grutas de Balankanché★**, and the ruins at **Yaxuná** and **Ek Balam**. *See Nature and Cenotes; Colonial Cities, Mayan Cities; Outdoor Activities; Shopping; Kids; Must Relax.*

EMERALD COAST★★

Some 80km/50mi north of Valladolid and Chichén Itzá is the Emerald Coast, home to flamingos and whale sharks. The town of **Río Lagartos** is a picturesque fishing village that lies on the edge of the **Reserva de la Biósfera de Ría Lagartos★★**, set aside in 1979 to protect the nesting grounds of the largest pink flamingo population in North America.

After visiting **Valladolid★★** and the newly opened pre-Hispanic city of **Ek Balam** on Highway 295, continue North until you can go no further (some 80km/50mi from Valladolid). By bus you will arrive at the bus station on Calle 19, just east of the main street through Río Lagartos—Calle 10—which runs

toward the waterfront. Inquire at the **Isla Contoy Restaurant**, along the waterfront on the West side, about tours of the Ría Lagartos estuary in order to see the flamingos. Lodging is available in nearby **San Felipe**, another small fishing village 12km/7.4mi west of Río Lagartos.

Isla Holbox★★ – This island is said to have been founded by pirates who sought refuge here and intermarried with Mayan locals. Seven miles long and one mile wide, the island lies at the northernmost tip of the peninsula. Laid back and sandy, it is only just beginning to be discovered by world travelers. To **get there** from Valladolid, take Highway 180 east some 90km/56mi and turn off at the tiny crossroads in El Ideal. Head due north 100km/63mi on state Highway 5 (Quintana Roo) until you reach Chiquilá. Here a ferry runs to the island 10 times daily, charging $4 per person.

The most common way to get around the island, other than by foot, is in golf carts. Ask around for rides!

See Nature and Cenotes; Outdoor Activities; Sailing and Cruising.

Boats at Isla Holbox

©Stuart Westmorland Photography

YUCATÁN AND WEST

BEACHES

The beaches of the states of Yucatán and Campeche do not boast the same tourist clamor of their Eastern Caribbean counterparts. Instead, they provide the same natural wealth, cultural intrigue and captivating history alongside an almost certain chance to swim or sun in a peaceful sea. These emerald green Gulf stream waters have brought the people of Yucatán a steady beating throughout history—from hurricanes to *conquistadores* to pirates seeking treasure—and are today home to all manner of intrigue and amusement for visitors.

Campeche Area

Peaceful **Playa Bonita★★** (*12.8km/ 8mi south of Campeche along Highway 180*) extends its soft white sands, actually made of finely crushed seashells, toward a calm sea ideal for wading, and has *palapas* for shade or snacks.

Celestún Beaches★★★

Between **Campeche★** and **Mérida★★** lies quiet **Celestún** (*take the Periferico out of Mérida toward Uman, to Kinchil and then Celestún. At the terminal on calle 71 by 64 and 66, buses leave every hour from 5am, 2 hour trip, 31 pesos*), chosen residence of a large population of flamingos.

You can enjoy its wide empty beaches with the family or on your own, go fishing, or bird watching, or look for a local guide to take you out on the estuary.

Mérida Coast Beaches★★

Most people seeking beach time from **Mérida★★** drive 45 minutes to **Progreso** (*21 mi/34km North via Hwy 26*). The port is new to the tourist scene and still maintains its local Mexican charisma. Its *malecon*, ideal for a stroll, lays along a broad white sand **beach** whose waters are calm and clear for swimming. Find shade beneath a *palapa* and enjoy a beer while people watching. The four mile pier was built to host cruisers without sacrificing the shoreline's charm. These boats now dock on Tuesdays and Thursdays (*see Sailing and Cruising*).

Celestún Beach

Progreso Beach

Progreso is also a good point of departure for several eco-touring opportunities (*see Nature and Cenotes*). To the west try **Sisal** if you are looking to duck the crowds or walk into history, or **Chelem** for a quaint town with basic services and wide beaches. To the east visit **Chicxulub**, which has a growing social scene thanks to its increasing expat community. **Telchac Puerto** has many services, though a bank is not among them, and is a good base for visiting the small ruins of **Xcambo**. Nearby **Chuburná** (*15min west, combis leave from Progreso every ½ hour*) boasts a broad, quiet beach and a chance to tour mangroves and watch the birds go about their daily activities (*see Nature and Cenotes*).

Emerald Coast Beaches★★

The north shore of the peninsula is known as the **Emerald Coast**. Unique natural phenomena abound here where the Gulf of Mexico meets the Caribbean Sea. After visiting Valladolid and Ek Balam, make your way to **San Felipe** (*12km/7.4mi west of Río Lagartos*) if you are looking to camp on a quiet beach, but only if you are not traveling in summer months or *semana santa* (the last week before Easter). Otherwise you may find yourself surrounded by the boisterous calls of locals who are also enjoying these offshore sands and waters. The remote treasure **Isla Holbox★★** (*north from Valladolid on highway 180*) is a must see for those who want to step back in time. Arrive by ferry from the town of **Chiquilá**. The largest vehicles to be found in the village's sandy streets are golf carts. Come between June and September for a rare opportunity to swim with whale sharks. The island's 43km/26.7mi of broad white sand beaches can be explored on foot, horseback, golf cart, or sea kayak.

Ruins at Xcambo

BEACHES

NATURE AND CENOTES

Whether witnessing the awesome flight of pink flamingos, or the power of a beam of light that has bored its way through stone, these sights will delight your senses. The **cenotes** of the Yucatán (*see infobox under Cozumel and South*) in particular provide excellent 🤿 **snorkeling** and 🤿 **diving**.

Reserva de la Biósfera de Ría Celestún★★

There are many ways to explore this unique National Wildlife Refuge (*Southwest from Mérida at the end of Highway 25 (for information on getting there, see Beaches); open year round daily Mon–Sun 8am–5pm; $4*), best known for its spectacular flocks of American Flamingos. You can arrive on foot to many sites here, but 🤿 **boat tours** are the best way to get around. The *lancheros* working at the Celestún dock give guided tours of the estuary (*$25*). See the flamingos and the "Isla de Pájaros" where cormorants, frigatebirds, and great egrets nest. Fishermen's tours (up to 8 people) tend to take in the **Ojo de Agua** freshwater spring for a swim, or head further south to a petrified mangrove forest and the ghost town of "Real de Salinas". Check out **EarthFoot Ecotours** (*www.earthfoot.org*), for birding tours with local expert David Bacab, or night tours where you will be looking for crocodiles and their nocturnal cohort with Feliciano Pech. **Ecoturismo Yucatán** (*www.ecoyuc.com*) has a day-tour from Mérida including guide, transportation and boat tours.

Mérida Area

Just a stone's throw from Progreso is the lovely ecotourism project at **Ría Chelem** (*40km/24.8mi north of Mérida*) where boats and guides are for hire to tour the estuary's mangroves and their characteristic fauna. The rides last 1.5–2hrs and end with a swim in the **ojo de agua Ixha**. You can arrange your 🤿 **tour** with the local fisherman's collective. Find them just south of the town's central plaza. The newly formed **Red de Ecoturismo de Yucatán A.C.** (*Calle 56-A no. 437 x 29, Edificio Cristal, Local 9, Paseo Montejo. www.redecotourismo.com*) is a good place to start your eco-adventures from Mérida.

Cenote Xlacah★, at the western end of the main sacbé leading out of **Dzibilchaltún** (*see Mayan Cities*), is clear and lovely for a dip after walking the ruins. It is also inhabited by six species of fish native to the Yucatán, three of which are only found in this cenote.

At **El Corchito** (*35km/21.7mi north of Mérida, 1km/.6mi from the highway to Chicxulub Puerto*), you can see various species of mangrove as you swim in one of the four ojos de agua, one of which, "helechos", is only 1m deep (perfect for kids).

Izamal Area

North from Izamal is **Oxwatz Eco-archeological Park** (*In Tekal de Venegas, 73km/45.3mi from Mérida. www.oxwatz.com*). This "eco-archeological park" is a local village's effort to retain their homelands and develop sustainably. To arrive you must walk or bike 13km/8mi down a sacbé (Mayan road). The tours, most of which last from six to eight hours, include birdwatching, snorkeling and diving in cenote **Kukulá**, a visit to unrestored **Xbaatún**, and camping.

Valladolid Area

The most famous cenote of all is at **Chichén Itzá★★★** but you cannot swim in it (*See Mayan Cities*). Breathtaking **Cenote Dzitnup ★★★** (*4km/2.4mi west of Valladolid off highway 180, open year round daily 7am–7pm, $2–$3*), also called **Xkeken**, is one of the few cenotes in Yucatán state to preserve most of its roof. You descend from its entrance into the large cave that houses this hidden swimming hole, which, at the right time of day, glows turquoise blue beneath the shaft of light that seeps through the ceiling to the cool water. **Cenote Samula★★**, (*daily 8am–5pm, $2–$3*) just down the road, is less developed but no less impressive. You may well find yourself alone as you admire the roots of a tree reaching into its waters. 6km/4mi from Chichén Itzá, the **Grutas de Balankanché★** were Mayan cermonial caverns, while **Cenote Ik-Kil★★** (*3km/1.8 mi from Chichén Itzá, 8am–6pm, $3–$4*) has sacred waters, now inside an eco-archeological park. You will hear the steady stream of waterfalls as you swim among the many fish. **Mayan Tours** (*1-877-482-3758, www.mayantours.com*) provides tours to these cenotes and other area sites of interest.

Ría Lagartos★★

(*North from Valladolid on Hwy 295*) This Biosphere Reserve covers the northernmost tip of the Yucatán. This is where flamingos spend their time when they are not in Celestún. Boat tours through the estuary snake around mangrove labyrinths and are a birdwatcher's delight. **Río Lagartos Expeditions** (*reserve boats and guides at the Restaurante Isla Contoy on the west side of Río Lagartos town's waterfront. www.riolagartosexpeditions.com*) provide estuary nature tours, fishing tours and a boat service to **Isla Holbox**.

Isla Holbox★★

At the northernmost tip of the peninsula and almost rounding the corner toward **Cancún★★** is **Isla Holbox** (*turn north off Hwy 180 onto Hwy 5 at the tiny town of El Ideal*), whose waters are part of the offshore **Biósfera de Yum Balam★★**. The island is best known for seeing its peaceful whale sharks (Jul–mid-Sept), which you will find basking in the sun near the surface.

Wet Set Dive Travel (*Av. 38 Nte., Lote 3, Manzana 200, between 1a and 5a Av., Playa del Carmen, www.wetsetdivetravel.com*) will pick you up at your hotel in **Cancún★★** or **Playa del Carmen★★** and return you afterwards. If you make it here on your own, look to Holbox Tours and Travel (*on Calle Bravo in front of the Playa, www.holboxwhalesharktours.com*) for a local guide, captain, and an hour or so out at sea.

©MAlbuquerque/iStockphoto.com

Cenote Dzitnup near Valladolid

COLONIAL CITIES

As Francisco de Montejo and his men marched north and then east on the sacbés laid out centuries before for Mayan elite, they picked apart the temples they encountered and built their homes and churches with the stones. The colonial cities they erected are today's World Heritage Sites, peaceful cobblestoned centers of arts and music that promise to delight their visitors.

MUST SEE YUCATÁN & WEST

CAMPECHE★

One of the first arrival grounds of the Spaniards, this city bore witness to battle upon battle between the native population and the Europeans, and then with pirates who sought the wealth of the port. The first 150 years of its written history are beset by these woes, until Spain conceded to the appeals of its people and began construction of the city's fortifications, most of which remain today. Your tour of the area will most likely not venture too far outside **La Muralla★**, the city's great wall. Construction of the wall, which marks a perimeter of 2.5km/1.5mi with gates facing the cardinal directions, began in 1686.

Cathedral, Campeche

©Catcha/Dreamstime.com

The defensive structure included eight bastions, of which seven remain. Today, they are host to a series of fascinating museums.

Getting There & Around

You can fly to Campeche, on the Gulf of Mexico, arriving at Campeche Airport, which lies 10km/6.2mi southeast of the city. A taxi to the center should cost around $9.

For a better airfare, try flying to **Cancún★★** or **Mérida★★** and travelling by land to Campeche. By bus you will most likely arrive at the first class ADO Terminal, 5km/3.1mi from the center on Avenida Central. A taxi will cost $4. By car you will arrive via Highway 180 North from Villahermosa or south from Mérida. The city center lies within the walls of the colonial fortress. For a guided tour of the city take the *tranvía*. It departs from the Plaza Principal every hour on the hour, and costs $7.

Old City★

Begin your walking tour on the **Plaza Principal**. On the northwest corner (seaward) of the plaza is the **Baluarte de la Soledad★** (*Calle 8., Campeche; Mon–Sun 8am–8pm; $2–$3; 981-816-8179*). It is home to the **Baluarte de la Soledad Museum of Maya Stelae**, reinaugurated in 2005, which boasts a fine collection

Fuerte de San Miguel, Campeche

©Yucatán Today

of unearthed Mayan lore from the many sites draped behind Campeche's thick jungle. From the upper level terrace enjoy views of the city center and orient yourself for further exploration. Also on the plaza, opposite the Cathedral, is the **Casa no.6 Centro Cultural** (*Calle 57 no.6, on the Plaza*), a 16th century mansion believed to have been home to Francisco de Montejo. Today it showcases baroque furniture and accessories typical to those used by the ruling class families who inhabited these spaces. Enquire here for tourist information.

Four blocks west on lovely Calle 10 and one block toward the water is the **Baluarte de San Carlos**, home to the **Museo de la Ciudad** (*Circuito Baluartes con Av. Justo Sierra Tue–Sat 9am–8pm, Sun 9am–1pm, $2–$3*). This bastion is the city's oldest, apt home to Campeche's City Museum. The museum has a model of the city in its fortressed heyday, along with the ships that used to fill its harbor. The roof gives another lovely view of the now peaceful Gulf of Mexico. Walk

back along the *malecón*, where you can breathe the salty Gulf air as you approach the **Baluarte de Santiago** (*Av. 16 de Septiembre and Calle 49*). With the completion of this bastion in 1704, the fortification of the city was complete. Today it welcomes visitors to the **Jardín Botánico Xmuch'haltun**, a small but abounding botanical garden with over 250 plant and tree species native to these tropical lands.

In the evening walk landward four blocks on Calle 57 to the **Puerta de Tierra★** (*Calle 59 y Calle 18, Circuito Baluartes con Av. Gobernadores, daily 8am–9pm, $1; Sound and Light Show Tue, Fri, Sat 8:30pm, $4*) where you will find a small museum that brings you face to face with yesterday's rulers and their pirate foes. Their weaponry is also on display. The **sound and light show** draws you into this period of the city's history. A short drive south of the walled city is the imposing hilltop fortress of **Fuerte de San Miguel★** (*follow the coast south on Av. Ruiz Cortines, after 2.5km/1.5m, turn left and continue 300m/325yd on*

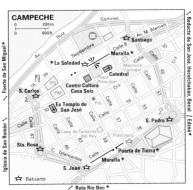

CAMPECHE

0   200m
0   600ft

COLONIAL CITIES

107

the Ruta Escenica; open year round Tue–Sun 8am–8pm; 981-816-5593; $2–$3). Begun at the end of the 18C, the fort completed the city's fortifications and was one of its most important defenses. It was taken by General Santa Anna in 1842 and used to plan maneuvers against separatists. The original moat, drawbridge, lookout towers and cannons speak of a militarized past. San Miguel is home to the **Museo Arqueológico**, recently renovated, which exhibits the awesome artistry of the original inhabitants of these lands. A burial scene with striking jade masks is displayed, which was unearthed in **Calakmul★★** (see Cozumel and South). The view of the **city★** and sea from the roof is spectacular.

MÉRIDA★★

If you come to Yucatán state's capital at the right time of year (in Spring), you will find "the White City" dressed in the burning red orange and bright yellow blossoms of flamboyan and lluvia de oro (rain of gold) trees, in striking contrast with the city's whitewashed colonial facades.

Getting There & Around

The White City lies just inland from the western and northern shores of the peninsula, some 200mi west of **Cancún★★**. You can fly into the Mérida International Airport, which lies 7km/4.3mi southwest of the city. Taxis at the transport desk outside charge $135 to take you to the Plaza Mayor. If you come by bus you will arrive at the Terminal CAME on Calle 70 between 69 and 71. A taxi to the plaza will charge $4.

Walking around the center is easy and enjoyable. The city follows a grid pattern; even streets run north–south and odd streets run east–west. Horse-drawn taxis line up on the plaza in the evenings and are a traditional way to take in the city's sites, sounds and smells at one of its liveliest hours.

Plaza Mayor (Plaza Grande)

Calles 60, 61, 62 and 63.

Mérida's main square (plaza mayor) was the city's heart long before the Spaniards arrived to dismantle its pyramids and build churches and homes. Framed by restaurants and shops dressed in the vestiges of a grandiose yesteryear, the park is home to numerous vendors and shaded by greenery. Couples will like the square's love seats. Go on Sunday to enjoy **Mérida en Domingo★**, sure to delight children of all ages.

The **Cathedral** (corner of Calle 60 and 61; open daily 6am–noon, 4pm–7pm) is the oldest on the American continent, and was built on the temple of **Ichcansihó**, or **T'ho**, using its stones. The Christ of the Blisters in the northeastern chapel got its name when it miraculously survived a fire that destroyed the church where it stood. To the right facing the park is the **Museo del Arte Contemporáneo Ateneo de Yucatán (MACAY)** (Calle 60 between 61-A and 63, just south of the cathedral; open year round Wed–Mon 10am–6pm (Fri, Sat 8pm); $2; 999-928-3258). The museum of contemporary art is housed in the 17C palace of the Archbishop. The upper level shows the work of Yucatecán painters and artisans. Continuing a clockwise stroll around the park's perimeter you will come to the **Casa de Montejo** (*Calle 63, #506, south side of the square*). Built by Francisco de Montejo of stones from the temples of T'ho, this mansion belonged to his kin from 1549 until it was sold to Banamex in 1980. Look closely at the **facade★**. Carved by the sweat and skill of native hands, this monument shows the Montejo coat of arms. The men at its sides are Montejo's victorious countrymen standing on the heads of the fallen Maya.

At the northwest corner of the square is the **Palacio Municipal** (*Calle 62*). The melon colored municipal palace is home to the square's clock and bell tower. The bell has not sounded for decades, but the building with its arcades is

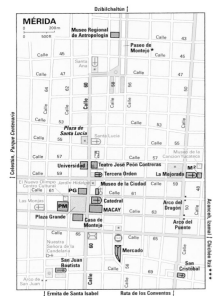

MÉRIDA

Palacio Municipal, Mérida

©Ignacio Guevara/Mexico Tourism Board

one of Mérida's defining faces and a landmark for orienting yourself in the city center. The **Casa del Alguacil** (*east side of the square*) is another conquistador's mansion, and subsequent home to various of the white city's elite families. Today the mansion and its arcade house eateries, an artisan shop, money exchange and the **Dulcería y Sorbetería Colón** (*see Must Eat*), where you can find yourself one of those ice cream cones you see everyone around you enjoying.

Finally, do not miss a chance to walk into the **Palacio de Gobierno** (*Calle 61, north side of the square; open daily 8am–8pm; closed national holidays*). The elegant governmental palace provides the backdrop for a series of aggressive **murals★** painted by *yucateco* Fernando Castro Pacheco

Salon with mural paintings, Palacio de Gobierno

©Ignacio Guevara/Mexico Tourism Board

in the 1970's. They depict the cosmology and violent history of the peninsula in striking hues. The palace is home to Yucatán state's governmental offices.

The recently re-opened **Museo de la Ciudad** (*Calle 56 between 65 and 65A. Follow Calle 60 south one block from the plaza, turn left on Calle 65; open Tue–Fri 8am–8pm, Sat–Sun 10am–2pm; guided tours in English, Spanish or French are complimentary*) is in a recently renovated building that was once the federal palace and later the post office. Covering pre-Hispanic to modern life in and around the white city, the museum boasts many articles of local import and intrigue among its collection.

Calle 60

North of the Plaza Mayor

After a walk around the Plaza Mayor, head north from the cathedral on Calle 60, which will lead you to peaceful café-lined plazas, colonial buildings and handicraft shops. On the first block you will come to the **Parque Cepada Peraza** (*Calle 60 at 59*), a favorite haunt for Mérida's student crowd. This park, also known as Parque Hidalgo, dates

back to the city's beginnings. It is an ideal place to read a book or enjoy a treat beneath the shade of almond trees.

Across Calle 50 is the **Iglesia de Jesús**. Of the Jesuit order, the Church of Jesus was built out of the Mayan temple that once stood here. Standing in the park on the west side of the church you can see carvings on two of these pre-Hispanic bricks. Be sure to peak inside the church as well.

Next door is Mérida's principal theater, the **Teatro José Peon Contreras**, named for Yucatán state's most distinguished symphony musician. Built in a French neoclassical style in the heyday of the henequen (fibrous agave used to make rope and twine) boom and the *porfiriato* (the period of rule by controversial dictator Porfirio Díaz, late 19C–early 20C), the theater today displays plastic arts in its wide lobby.

Across the street is the **Universidad de Yucatán**. The Jesuit (or Third) Order built this entire block in 1618. When the Jesuits were expelled from Spain and its empire (1767) they left behind the roots of an educational institution; today's highly respected University of Yucatán. The university's Ballet Folklórico runs a colorful traditional performance on the central patio Friday nights at 9pm (*$3*). Another block north lies the lovely **Parque Santa Lucia** (*Calle 60 at 55*), once the city's stagecoach station. The park now hosts a weekly serenade of Trova Yucatecá on Thursday nights at 9pm. A *Bazar de Artesanías*, or local handicrafts market, is held here on Sundays. Walking three blocks further north will bring you to the **Parque Santa Ana** (*Calle 60 at 45*), a modern park that marks a good turning point from Calle 60 toward the Paseo de Montejo. After strolling the open space, walk on to the right then take the second left to continue this walking tour.

Paseo de Montejo★★

Starting at Calle 47, going north.

Built at the turn of the 20C to emulate the Champs Elysées in Paris, this fashionable paseo is lined with lavish homes. The houses were built by those who reaped the benefits of the region's henequen boom. Although many of the homes were sold following the bust of the 'green gold,' most remain intact and some even renovated. Today they house upscale restaurants, clubs and hotels. The **Museo Regional de Antropología★** (*Paseo de Montejo at Calle 43; open year round Tue–Sat 8am–8pm, Sun 8am–2pm; $3–$4*) is housed in **Palacio Cantón**—an imposing mansion that was built at the beginning of the 20C for Francisco Cantón Rosado, local magnate and politician who was linked with then dictator Porfirio Díaz. The museum's halls present

Palacio Cantón

© Maria De Lourdes Alonso/Mexico Tourism Board

an overview of pre-Hispanic culture, covering agriculture, social evolution, trade, mathematics, sacrifice and burial rituals.

At the end of Paseo de Montejo is the **Monumento a la Bandera**, 'Memorial to the Flag.'

Outside the Center

Hacienda Sotuta de Péon

45min south of Mérida, take Periférico exit 4, Calle 42 Sur. $250 adults, $210 kids.

At this hacienda you are invited to experience life in the henequen boom. The working hacienda provides a two and a half hour tour of their facilities in traditional horse-drawn trucks, and includes a visit to a Mayan homestead, and to a neighboring cenote.

Monumento a la Bandera

© Maura Reap/Dreamstime.com

Hacienda Yaxcopoil★★

Follow the Periférico to Carr. 180 south, at Uman take Carr. 261 south to Km186. En-route to Uxmal and the Ruta Puuc. Open Mon–Sat 9am–6pm, Sun 9am–1pm. $5–$6. 999-900-1193. www.yaxcopoil.com.

Now representing only three percent of its original size (22,000 acres), this plantation, founded in the 17C, was once one of the most important rural estates in the Yucatán. In Mayan Yaxcopoil means "the place of the green alamo trees", the name in fact inherited from nearby Mayan ruins. The Neo-Classical hacienda-**museum** includes the *casa principal*'s spacious lounges, drawing rooms and gardens, a chapel, an orchard, a well, farming machinery, storehouses, workshop and infirmary.

VALLADOLID★★

The third peninsular city founded by Francisco de Montejo (this one in 1543), Valladolid was built atop pre-Hispanic **Zací**. In the 19C these streets were scene to some of the bloodiest battles of the Caste Wars. Today, quaint colonial Valladolid is a picturesque provincial town full of colonial and 19C buildings.

Begin your tour on the plaza, where women are likely to be hawking their colorful *huipiles* (traditional back-strap woven blouses). On Sunday evenings at 8pm couples dance to *danzón* around the square's bandstand. Next to the Cathedral of San Gervasio is the **Palacio de Gobierno**. See the city's history painted in the murals by local artist Manuel Lizama, exhibited on the second floor. More of his murals can be found one block east of the plaza on Calle 41 at the **Museo San Roque**, where you will also find some of the treasures recently uncovered at **Ek-Balam** (*see Mayan Cities*). One block north and another east is **Cenote Zací**. Finally, two blocks west of the plaza on Calle 41 you will come across Calle 41-A, called **Calle de los Frailes**. Walk southwest along this lovely colonial roadway to the **Iglesia de San Bernardo de Sisal**, built by the Franciscans in the 1552 amidst controversy. It looks like a fortress, attesting to the social climate that surrounded Catholic authorities in the area.

Colorfully painted houses of Valladolid

© Franck Camhi/BigStockPhoto.com

MAYAN CITIES

The Mayab is still home to the husks of the ancient world's great cities. Many are connected to this day by the main thoroughfares (sacbés) used by ruling dynasties and shamans whose tombs have been unearthed in recent times. These cities of stone are sculpted tributes to the grandeur of the gods of yore. Here you will find Chaac, Kinich Ahau and Iztamná in wait, keeping watch over white sands and limestone.

CHICHÉN ITZÁ★★★

The ancient city is set in the middle of a vast plain between Mérida and Cancún, alongside the village of Pisté. You can get there by car heading east out of Mérida on the toll road 75 miles to the town of Pisté. If you wish to go by bus, the ADO terminal on Calle 50 at 67 has services every hour for $5–$6. Take Carr. 180 East. After 69km/43mi, in Kantunil, take either the toll road or continue on the freeway to the town of Pisté. Pick up a map of the site before entering at the visitor center. Entry fee $9–$10, including the one hour 🎆 *sound and light show (7pm Fall/Winter, 8pm Spring/Summer). Guides $45.*

Chichén, meaning "at the mouth of the well", pre-dates the **Itzá** people (Chontal Maya for 'water sorcerers'), who arrived from Campeche and the **Río Bec★★** region (*see Cozumel and South*) in the late 8C–early 9C. The religious center this commercial seafaring people developed is known today as **Chichén Viejo**. The 9C saw decline throughhout the Mayan region, but a new period of building began at Chichén from the 10C–12C in **Toltec** style (**Chichén Nuevo**). Toltec deities appear in iconography, such as Tlaloc, the rain god, in place of Chaac. The central Mexican Toltecs had inherited the feathered serpent god,

Quetzalcoatl from the people of Teotihuacán (near Mexico city, abandoned in 7C) and brought his story to Chichén, where he appears in the form of **Kukulcán**. According to myth, the god Quetzalcoatl was expelled from the Toltec capital of Tula, leaving for the east, which many interpret as evidence of Toltec civil war. Certainly the rise of Toltec culture at Chichén indicates settlement by people from this kingdom. The theocracy of this period was militarized and practiced Toltec-style human scarifice. Toward the end of the **12C**, a league of nations with **Mayapán★** and **Uxmal★★★** ended with war, precipitating the decline and abandonment of mighty Chichén Itzá.

The city is comprised of two main groups of structures from the two main periods of construction. As you enter at the main entrance, pick up a site map and enter **Chichén Nuevo** beside the **Gran Juego de Pelota**. The Great Ball Court (*see ballcourt infobox, Cozumel and South*) is 166m/545ft long by 69m/225ft wide. In the sloping gallery that makes up its lateral walls—covered in stone carvings featuring bloody scenes from games past—whispers at one end are clearly audible at the other, and claps or shouts echo nine times, a sacred number for this city's people.

MUST SEE

Templo de los Guerreros (Temple of the Warriors), Chichén Itzá

© Angelika Stern/iStockphoto.com

Another auditory mystery is contained in the epic **Pirámide de Kukulcán★★★** (see p7), also called "**El Castillo**," which lies southeast of the Ball Court past the **Templo de los Jaguares** and the sacrificial platforms known as **Tzompantli**, whose base depicts decapitated skulls, and the **Plataforma de Águilas y Jaguares**, carved with eagles and serpents devouring human hearts.

Kukulcán's pyramid has nine sharp levels and four staircases that begin their ascent with the head of a serpent and end with its tail at a simple square temple. At sunset on the Equinox the play of shadows is such that the serpent can be seen ascending one side of the pyramid and descending the other, disappearing into the grassy plaza near the Ball Court.

If you clap your hands on the steps—ask if they can be climbed—the sound you hear is remarkably like the call of a quetzal, Mayan holy bird and one of the symbolic personifications of Quetzalcoatl/Kukulcán. Though recently explained as the physics of periodic reflections from the faces of the steps, the phenomenon is awesome. This temple,

highly influenced by Toltec styles, is superimposed upon a series of smaller temples, each built over the other so as to contain it without destroying it. Inside is a **throne★★** in the form of a jaguar, painted red and spotted with jade. Inquire as to whether the inner stairs are open.

North of the Castillo, past the **Plataforma de Venus**, symbolic of Quetzalcoatl in his form as the morning star, is a sacbé that leads 300m to the **Cenote Sagrado**. The Sacred Cenote is the likely namesake of Chichén, and surely supplied the city with its most precious of resources. Modern dredgings of its depths have turned up a wealth of offerings—including human remains, jade and gold disks—thrown into the well. It is said that those who returned to the surface were lauded as seers who had communed with the gods. An impressive 60m in circumference, this near perfectly round sinkhole was thought to be the entrance to the *Inframundo*.

To the East from the Castillo is the **Templo de los Guerreros**, beautifully carved with the bellicose figures of Toltec influence and crowned by a Chac Mool statue.

114

Along with the adjoining **Grupo de las Mil Columnas**, these are the most reminiscent structures of the city of Tula.

Chichén Viejo comprises the south end of the site, accessible both from the quieter eastern entrance as well as a path that leads from the great plazas of Chichén Nuevo. Its buildings are clearly related to those in the Puuc hills, and its softer ceremonial nature remains highly sacred to contemporary Maya. These buildings, except **El Osario** which is the first pyramid you will encounter from the north, were built in the Classic period, before the arrival of Itzá and Toltec influences. The **Caracol** (snail) is an observatory that is so precise it baffles even modern astronomers. From here the wisdom behind the Mayan calendar was slowly accrued from the heavens. The **Edificio de las Monjas** houses a group of Chaac masks that together make one larger mask whose mouth is a doorway. Another vital source of water, **Cenote Xtoloc**, is found within Chichén Viejo and has a recently restored temple on its edge.

Ek-Balam

In the Chichén Itzá area, 28km/ 17.5mi northeast of Valladolid. Open 9am–5pm. $2–$3.

A series of defensive walls surround the ceremonial center of what was once the large settlement of Ek-Balam, or "black jaguar". Thought to have been a powerful force at its height in the Late Classical period, due to the sacbés that lead out from it in all directions, Ek-Balam is a relatively recent discovery and among the lesser visited sites in the area. Come here to see the process of archeology in motion. What has been uncovered is already remarkable, and what remains hidden is intriguing. Be sure to climb the **Acropolis★**, where a masterful stucco figure guards the entrance to the underworld. There is a beautiful view from the top.

UXMAL★★★

80km/50mi from Mérida. Head southwest on Carr. 180 to Umán (18km/11mi); then take Carr. 261 south. Uxmal is 16km/10mi past **Muna** *(See Shopping). Open 8am–5pm (winter), 8am–6pm (summer); service open 8am–10pm. $9–$10*

North building of Cuadrangulo de las Monjas, Uxmal

©Carlos Sanchez/Mexico Tourism Board

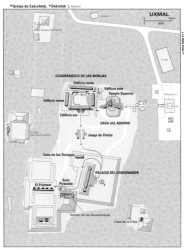

the construction, which contrary to legend has evidence of being built throughout hundreds of years in varying styles. A striking mask of Chaac provides entrance to the chamber through its mouth. Its western steps face the setting sun at the summer solstice, and also the **Cuadrangulo de las Monjas**.

Misnamed by the Spanish, who thought its rooms rendered a likeness to their convents, the nunnery consists of four buildings, one in each of the cardinal directions, which were built in the last decade of the 9C. Each of the four lies on different levels, and the complete complex forms a courtyard with exceptional acoustics. Uxmal like other Mayan centers would have been a center of learning and knowledge, so some argue that this 'convent' was some sort of school, whether military or academic. Regardless of its use, the square remains an ideal example of refined Mayan architectural skill. All four buildings are made of typically plain lower walls beneath highly decorated carved fretwork on the upper sections, whose repeated geometric and zoomorphic figures create a mesmerizing visual effect. The arched passageway of the south building leads to the Ball Court, and gives the impression of emerging from underground upon passing through it.

The **Palacio del Gobernador** is another exquisite example of Classic Mayan architecture, and its

(admission to the site and the sound & light show); $3 (admission to the sound & light show only).

This magical World Heritage Site is the quintessence of a highly refined Puuc-style architecture, with stunning ornate friezes. "Thrice built" Uxmal was a great metropolitan and religious center from the 7C to the 10C, at the close of the Classic period. It was abandoned around 1200 following war among regional powers. Relatively little archeological research has been conducted here so little is known of its history.

The imposing **Casa del Adivino**, or Pyramid of the Magician, is an oval-shaped structure that rises 35m/115ft at a surprising angle. Legend says that it was built in one night by a dwarf, who then played a song and answered several riddles in order to be named king. A steep stairway leads to the **Upper Temple**, the fifth level of facade should not be missed. Also on the platform of the Palace is the **House of the Turtles**, named for the turtles of different shapes and sizes that decorate it. For the Maya the turtle represents the creation of this world, as well as its center.

The **Gran Pirámide** consists of nine levels that culminate in the **Templo de las Guaca-mayas**, named for the macaws that adorn its façade, which are related to Kinich the god of the sun. The **view★★** from the top is spectacular.

Do not miss the 🔊**sound and light show** displayed nightly, which relates a (disputed) history of Uxmal as it plays light in the shadows of the masterful carvings for a marvelous visual effect.

RUTA PUUC★

The Ruta Puuc is a chain of Mayan sites south of Mérida, near Uxmal.

The sprinkling of sites that spread across these rare hills flourished during the Late Classic period, from AD600–900. The ceremonial centers are the namesake of the "Puuc architectural style", which includes the Mayan arch and ornate stucco friezes, often of Chaac the rain god, among its signatures.

Another commonality among these sites is the lack of natural cenotes and subsequent use of massive cisterns. This, perhaps, explains the abundance of detail dedicated to Chaac.

The sites comprise one of the highest densities of ancient centers in the Americas, giving a quiet and majestic feel for life past.

©S. Greg Panosian/iStockphoto.com
Facade of the Codz Pop (Temple of the Masks), Kabáh

Kabáh★

23km/14.3mi from Uxmal. Go east on Carr. 261 for 15km/ 9.3mi to Santa Elena, then continue another 8km/5mi south. Open daily 8am–5pm. $3–$4.

Named for the "Lord of strong and powerful arm", Kabáh is connected to Uxmal by an 18km/11.1mi sacbé marked by an impressive **arch★**, 10m/32.8ft tall, which can be seen across the highway from the bulk of the site's excavated ruins. The **Codz Pop★★★**, whose awesome western facade is decked in more than 100 identical masks of Chaac, is the most famous of these.

Sayil★

9km/5.6mi from Kabah. Go south and at 5km/3mi turn left. Sayil is 4km/2.5mi down this road. Open daily 8am–5pm. $3–$4.

The **Palacio★** of the quiet ruins at Sayil, or "house of the ants", boasts elaborate friezes honoring Chaac and Ah Mucen Cab, god of bees and honey. It is easy to imagine the grandeur of yore standing beneath this magnificently crafted palace, looking out along the sacbé that leads from its steps.

Less excavated structures dot the jungle, and a sweaty walk through the woods may be rewarding.

Xlapak

5km/3mi from Sayil. Open daily 8am–5pm. $2–$3.

The smallest of the Ruta Puuc sites, whose name means "touching walls", Xlapak is also known for its ornate Palacio, which honors Chaac with three rows of masks at each of its entrances.

Labná★

4km/2.5mi from Xlapak. Open daily 8am–5pm. $3–$4.

Labná was probably a subsidiary settlement of a larger politcal structure, with Uxmal or Sayil as its capital. Traces of human occupation at Labná, "old house", date back to the 1C AD, but the main structures date to AD750–1000. It's **Palacio★** boasts an ornate image of a human face emerging from the mouth of a snake. The **Arco★★** that lies to the south along the well-preserved sacbé is an elaborate and elegant model of this Mayan architectural trait. 18km/8.7mi northeast of Labná are the **Grutas de Loltún★★** (stone's flower), a twelve cavern system nearly 2km/1.2mi long, first inhabited by man as early as 3,000BC.

IZAMAL★

From Mérida, drive East on Highway 180 to the Kantunil exit. Go 17km/10.5mi North to Izamal.

"The place of Itzamná", the Mayan creator of life and mythical founder of this city, was once a great ceremonial center dedicated to the gods of healing. The base of the pyramid **Kinich-Kak-Mo** or "fire macaw—face of the sun", is the third largest in Meso-America. It sustained abuse at the hands of the Catholic Church, but has been partially restored and has a stunning view of the area from the top. Legend has it that offerings to the Great Earth Monster left atop this pyramid were collected by the god in the form of a macaw. You can also visit the **Convento de San Antonio de Padua**, built in the 16C by Bishop Landa atop the city's most important pyramid in an attempt to placate the native religious vigor that characterized this special part of cities. The statue of the Virgin Mary is one of the most venerated in all of Mexico, though many believe that the miracles she is said to perform outdate both her presence and that of the church she represents. Locals and tourists alike get around by horse-drawn carriage in the modern artsy town of Izamal.

MAYAPÁN★

Head southeast from Izamal (see above) on Carr. 18 until reaching Acanceh, 20km/12.4mi; continue south for another 19km/11.8mi, following the "Zona Arqueológica Mayapán" signs. Open daily 8am–5pm. $27.

Post-Classic (12–15C) Mayapán at its height led a confederation of city states including **Uxmal★★★** and **Chichén Itzá★★★** for almost two centuries. This ended when the city, surrounded by a protective wall 9.7km/6mi long, attacked its allies. Mayapán was briefly the leading political and military force, before it too was broken by its enemies and abandoned. Mayapán's buildings exemplify changing influences in architecture and lifestyle with the arrival of the Toltec to Puuc lands.

Twice a year at the equinox, Kukulcán can be seen descending the steps of Mayapán's **Castillo**. It also exhibits carvings of eagles, serpents and warriors, and is home to a **Caracol** observatory.

The quiet of this site makes for a pleasant visit among the stones.

EDZNÁ★

55km/34mi east from Campeche on Hwy 180. At Chiná turn left onto Hwy 188 another 10km/6mi. Open daily 8am–5pm, $3–$4. Luz of the Itzaes **sound and light Show** *Fri and Sat, 7pm.*

Edzná means "House of the Itzaes," and housed Chontal or Itzá priests, merchants, and craftsman at its peak between AD600–900, when its temples were plastered with red stucco that can still be traced on some of its buildings. Its architecture shows influence from each of the peninsula's styles: Puuc, Chenes, Río Bec and Peten. The system for rainwater collection in the valley, which lies beneath the flood plain, is ingenious.

The imposing **Templo de Cinco Pisos★★** features styles typical to both palaces and temples. A small ritual platform lying at its base is still used by a local shaman to bid the rains to fall. Do not miss the **Templo de los Mascarones**, on the Pequeña Acropolis behind the ball court, where the two faces (rising and setting) of Kinich Ahau, the sun-god, are protected beneath a thatched roof.

© Pagliara Filippo/Bigstockphoto.com

Templo de Cinco Pisos (Temple of Five Stories), Edzná

DZIBILCHALTÚN

20km/12.4mi from Mérida. Take Carr. 261 north and at 15km/9.3mi turn right 5km/3.1mi to Dzibilchaltún. Open daily 9am–5pm. $5–$6. 999-924-9495.

Upon entering the "old house", the longest occupied of all Mayan sites, starting before 1,000BC, you are greeted by the **Museo del Pueblo Maya★** (*Open Tue–Sun 9am–4pm*), which traces the Mayan people through to modern times. Currently home to the seven dolls that name the site's **Templo de las siete muñecas**, it also displays other local findings. The huge site, spread throughout low jungle in an ecological park, provides little descriptive information, so consider hiring a guide at the main entrance.

Aké, the archeological site and adjacent working henequen hacienda, is on the back road that leads east out of Mérida toward **Izamal★** via Chacalchen. An anomaly for many Mayanists, this site may make you feel that you've wandered into a land of giants. After walking the ruins, be sure to visit the **hacienda**, which still produces sisal fiber in much the same way it did more than a century ago.

OUTDOOR ACTIVITIES

Despite the heat and humidity, the Yucatán will beckon you out of doors to explore beneath its sun. These lands entice adventurers both new and old with any number of activities.

DIVING TRIPS

Ría Lagartos Expeditions (*www.riolagartosexpeditions. com*) provides transportation and waiting service to certified divers who wish to explore the reserve's coral reefs, blue holes where fresh and salt water collide in swirling schools of fish, and even shipwrecks. They do not provide equipment or certification. **EcoTurismo Yucatán** (*www. ecoyuc.com*) provide diving trips to **Arrecife Alacranes**, a coral reef 62 nautical miles north of Progreso, where you can dive among the wrecks. The four-day, three-night expedition is available Apr–Sept. You can also enquire about diving on these reefs at the **Marina Silcer** in Progreso. **Mayan Lands** (*www.mayaneco tours.com—Spanish only*) will take you diving in the cenotes of **Abala**, (*40min south of Mérida off Hwy 180*).

GOLF

Located on the road from Mérida to Progreso, the **Club de Golf de Yucatán** (*www.golfyucatan. com*) has 18 holes at a par of 72, with 6,590 total yards. Also near to Progreso is **La Ceiba Golf and Country Club**, an 18-hole championship course designed by Jack Nicklaus. The par 72, 6,528 yard course features long fairways dotted by palm trees. Avid golfers should also keep tabs on the construction of **Flamingo Lakes Golf & Country Club Resort** (*Dzemul, Yucatán, 30min from Mérida. www.flamingolakegolfresort.com*), and the **Campeche Playa Golf Marina and Spa Resort** (*www. campechebeachresort.com*), halfway between Ciudad del Carmen and Campeche.

HORSEBACK RIDING

Ride on horseback to **Chichén Itzá★★★** like an archeologist of yore, tie up your horse and pick around the ruins on tours with the **Mayaland Hotel** (*tours from the Lobby at 7am, 1pm, 3:30pm; $60*). On **Isla Holbox★★** at **La Casa Maya de José Lima** (*in town on the North Beach, www.casa mayadejoselima.com*), you can find a mare to accompany you as you ramble across miles of white sands. In **Cuzamá** (*south of Mérida on Hwy 180, inquire about trucks at the old hacienda, $100 for four*) a horsedrawn truck, used in the past to move henequen around this hacienda, will lead you 9km/5.5mi

Fishing with seagulls in Celestún

© lucio42/Fotolia.com

to three cenotes, each unique and each ideal for a refreshing dip.

FISHING

The entire coast of Yucatán state promises to delight fishermen and women of all ilk, and while you can hire a boat and captain for jaunts at sea in any seaside populace, some spots are worth special mention. **Isla Holbox★★** boasts the unique attribute of resting near to **Cabo Catoche**, the northernmost point on the peninsula, where the emerald Gulf waters spill into the turquoise waters of the Caribbean. This means excellent fishing. Likewise, **Celestún** is home to such rich diversity of zoo- and phyto-plankton that it keeps the flamingos coming back year after year, and promises that a good catch lies beneath the surface.

BIKING

The bicycle may well prove the best way to explore the Yucatán. In Mérida you can rent one with **Eco-Turismo Yucatán** (*www.ecoyuc. com*) for $10 a day. The company also provides a guided cycling day tour into Mérida's environs. No cyclist should miss 🚴**cycling on Sunday in Mérida**. A new city program closes a large chunk of the center (*Paseo Montejo from Plaza de la Bandera to La Ermita church*) to car and bus traffic from 8am–noon. The **Bici-Ruta**, aside from calling all bicycles in the white city out for a romp in the subjugated streets, also provide activities for children, such as making piñatas, in the Plaza de la Bandera from 9am–11am. If you want a serious biking tour, be sure to look to **!El Tour** (*www.bikemexico. com*), for one of their excursions in Yucatán state.

🎈BALLOONING

EcoTurismo Yucatán (*www. ecoyuc.com.mx/daytours*) will take you into the skies to observe Chichén Itzá from above. The tour begins at 5am with transport from Mérida hotels to Chichén Itzá. The balloon ride lasts about an hour, depending on wind conditions, and is followed by a guided tour of both the Chichén Itzá and nearby Yaxunah. It includes a visit to a cenote for a swim. Minimum occupancy is five and maximum is 28 in three balloons. The trip costs $299.

Horseback rides along the sand

©Jason Allies/iStockphoto.com

SAILING AND CRUISING

The Gulf shores of the Yucatán Peninsula are dotted with ports both past and present. While **Campeche★**, Sisal and Telchac *puertos* perhaps witnessed more coming and going in days gone by, the port at **Progreso**, and the town itself, are just becoming known to the modern world of cruising and sailing. The shallow waters at Progreso allow its pier to extends surprisingly far into the calm sea, keeping the coastline comparatively free of cruise ship clutter. Winds from the northeast tend to blow between 12 and 15 knots year-round, aside from bouts during the hurricane season between June and November.

Watersports

Though the Gulf Stream, coupled with industrial traffic, along the coasts of Veracruz, Tabasco and Campeche, keep the off-shore deeps here free of cruisers, the shallow waters of the coastline are ideal for all manner of water sports. Sport Marina and Beach Club **Marina Silcer** in Progreso (*take Hwy 27 east out of Progreso toward Chicxulub, www.marinasilcer.com*) is the place to be if you want to get out onto the calm green sea. They rent Hobie Cats and equipment for kitesurfing, and also provide courses for children and adults in sailing Lasers and kitesurfing. **Windsurfing** is also available at Progreso.

Boat Hire/ Skippered Tours

In almost any coastal town you can hire a boat among local fishermen in order to explore off-shore or try your luck with the day's catch. Most will even know of an expert *cocinera* who can prepare it for you when you return to the mainland. Much of the shoreline is guarded by offshore spits that embrace mangrove-lined estuaries. These sanctuaries of biodiversity are now being exploited for tourism in a series of local ecotourism ventures. In **San Crisanto** (*18 miles east of Progreso on Hwy 27, offices one block from crossroads across from the baseball field. $3*), local fishermen sculpted the paths

Windsurfing in Progreso

©Yucatán Today

©Helen Filatova/BigStockPhoto.com

Cruise ship in Yucatán waters

their boats follow through the mangroves with their machetes. The half-hour 🦅 **tour** culminates in a dip in one of the area's newly uncovered cenotes. **Dzilam de Bravo** *(112km/69.6mi northwest of Mérida on Hwy 178, or east of San Crisanto by Hwy 27, 1-991-912-2520; inquire about tours with the Coop Dzayachuleb next to the Port Captain's office)* is a fishing village on the edge of a state reserve of the same name, where you can hire a tour to **Las Bocas**, where the fresh water that surges beneath meets the sea in underwater cenotes. Kayaking, camping and sportfishing are also available.

Cruising

The pier at **Progreso** has only recently opened to cruises and the adventures waiting at this undiscovered port of call are already delighting the different tastes of their new visitors. Beaches for sunning with rolling green waves for a swim, people watching on the *malecon* and excellent guacamole, are but only a splash of what awaits at landfall. Just beyond are day excursions in all directions and for all kinds. **Carnival Cruiselines**

(www.carnival.com) has five, six and seven-day itineraries that call at the port of Progreso. The fun ships Fantasy, Ecstasy and Valor *($279-$679)* depart from New Orleans, Mobile and Galveston. The cruises stop for eight or nine hours at Progreso, allowing for any number of organized or individual on-shore touring opportunities. The new visit to Dzibilchaltun followed by a break at the beach promises intrigue and leisure. Other tours will take you as far as Chichén Itzá and back in just seven hours. **Royal Caribbean** *(www.royalcaribbean.com)* has two five-day packages *($379-$849)* that depart from Tampa and call on **Progreso** and **Cozumel★★** *(see Cozumel and South)*. The ship docks from 7am till 4pm, allowing plenty of time for one of the 22 excursions provided by the company onshore. On the higher end, **Peter Deilmann Cruises** *(www.deilmann-cruises.com)* have a 15-night cruise *($6,320-$19,010)* starting in Baltimore and ending in Montego Bay, Jamaica, which will let you off at Progreso from 7am-7pm. Try www.lastcruises. com, or www.cruises.com.

SHOPPING

Even those who typically resist the draw of shopping may find themselves anxious to drop all and hit the shops as soon as they arrive. If you are looking for light clothes, a hat, or simply a taste of the color and artistry of the people of the Yucatán, you will not be disappointed here. From hammocks to replicas of ancient ceremonial vases, from flower-clad huipiles to miniature skeletons wallowing over their now-empty bottles, the Yucatán's markets and shops have what you need and what you may not even know you are looking for.

Mérida

See Colonial Cities.

If you are wondering where you can find the people of Mérida, check its 🛍 **Mercado Lucas de Gálvez** (*Calle 65 and 69 by 56 and 56 A, southeast of the Plaza Mayor*) for some local *chisme* (gossip). You can also look for handicrafts, new fruits to taste, chilies of all shapes and colors, hammocks, hats and leather goods. Actually, it has been said that this market has everything.

The nearby **Bazaar de Artesanías** (*Calle 56*), with its large-lettered sign, sells artisans' creations. Crafts

Weaving panama hats in a cave, Becal

©Mito Covarrubias/Ami-md/Mexico Tourism Board

hunters should also check the **Bazaar García Rejón** (*Calle 65, between calles 58 and 60*) and be sure to peek in at the state-run **Casa de Las Artesanias** (*Calle 63, between calles 64 and 66*) for a more select offering of original handicrafts. While you can find hammocks on many a street corner throughout the peninsula, many people look to **Hamacas El Aguacate** (*Calle 58 #604 x 73 01; 999-928-64-29*), which for more than 50 years has supplied this most indispensable of furnishings to residents and visitors of Mérida.You can also try the new **Mayan Hands** (*Calle 41*) for competitive prices.

Maya Chuy (*Calle 18B #80 at 15B, 1-999-981-4442*) is an embroidery coop that works with women from neighboring Mayan villages in an attempt at bringing them into a sustainable family economy. The store sells the fruits of their labor: women's, men's and children's apparel, bags, tablecloths and manta. To continue dressing the family, visit world-renowned **Guayaberas Jack** (*Calle 59 # 507A, between 60 and 62; 52 (999) 928-60-02*) for several signature variations of traditional Cuban garb, made the official attire of the Yucatán by those merchants of 'green gold' who sought its cool comfort for these climes.

El Sombrero Popular (*Calle 65 between 58 and 60*) can help to top off an ensemble or shade out the sun. Here you can find panama hats, named perhaps in part thanks to Teddy Roosevelt, who helped popularize the simple comfort and style of the Jipijapa hat he bought on a visit to the canal a century ago.

Izamal

See Mayan Cities; Ideas and Tours—Convent Route.
When you come to visit this magical blend of worlds past and present, be sure to ask in restaurants or hotels for a locally made map of **artisan's workshops**. You can even hire a horse-drawn carriage to take you! Also visit **Hecho a Mano** on the central plaza.

Ticul

Near Uxmal.
For Ceramics, **Arte Maya** (*Calle 23, #301, in Ticul along Highway 18, www.artemaya.com.mx*), along the **Ruta Puuc**, opens its doors to visitors who want to see how the ancient Maya worked the same materials with the same techniques to achieve the same artistic magnificence on display today.

Muna

This lovely colonial town half an hour from Mérida is a must stop for those visiting Uxmal who are interested in traditional artistry. Muna is home to the **Taller de Artesanías Los Ceibos** (*Calle 13 #201, 997-971-0036*), a world renowned family-run workshop that uses the materials and methods of their ancestors to craft pristine ceramic reproductions of the pieces archeologists and pirates alike

have removed from these lands. While best known for their work in ceramics, the family also sculpts wood, leather, stone and jade. The taller is adjoined to the restaurant Chun-Yaax-Che, which serves a delicious *pollo pibil* and exhibits the family's work in its gardens.

Campeche

See Colonial Cities.
In Campeche, the **Casa de Artesanías Tukulná** (*Calle 10 #333, www.tulkulna.com*), which in Mayan means "house of thought", houses exhibitions of, and sells handicrafts by, the state's artisans. Campeche also excels in its work in ceramics, embroidery, and the weaving of baskets, hammocks, and hats.
Be sure to visit **Becal** (*on Highway 180 halfway between Campeche and Mérida*) if you are interested in panama hats. Here you can ask local artisans for a look at their workshops, where you will likely be shown into an ancient natural or man-made cave out behind their houses. The Jipijapa palm used for weaving these hats, named for their birthplace in Ecuador, is much more pliable in the cool humidity found in the caves, allowing for a finer result.

Valladolid

See Colonial Cities.
The **Mercado Municipal** (*Calle 32 and 37*) is a good place to visit on Sunday mornings, and also to find delicious local honey and many further wonders. *Huipiles* and other local artisan ware can be found both in the city's peaceful Central Square as well as the **Mercado de Artesanías** (*corner of calles 39 and 44*).

FOR KIDS

Few places on earth provide as many opportunities for experiential learning as does the Yucatán. Colonial cities living modern lives next to millennial cities whose buildings still dance by the light of the sun; rivers that birth freshwater wells and salty estuaries where pelicans feed; the open and *alegre* culture of Mexico's people; all this and much more make this a prime destination for an unforgettable family holiday. Refer to the the following sections in this guide for:

Colonial/Mayan Cities

- **Mérida en Domingo** provides activities and fun for kids of all ages, both visitors and locals.
- **Museo de la Ciudad** in Mérida has activities for kids Saturday mornings from 9–11.
- The 🔥 **sound and light show** at the **Puerta de Tierra★** in Campeche is a fun and engaging way to get inside the city's history.
- **Fuerte de San Miguel★** in Campeche, with its stone fortifications, is perfect for imagining life under threat of pirate attacks.
- The tour at **Hacienda Peon de Sotuta** near Mérida will take you back to the days of hennequen production and delight your child with strange machinery.
- 🔥 **Sound and light shows** at **Uxmal★★★** and **Chichén Itzá★★★** brings the ancient Mayan civilization to life.

Nature and Cenotes

- **Celestún**, on the west coast is tranquil and full of nature with a wide, often empty, beach.

Outdoor Activities

- **Horseback riding** to Old Chichén will make your kids feel like explorers en route to a discovery.
- **Bici-Ruta** in Mérida fills the streets with bikes of all sizes and colors, with activities from 9am–11am.

- Swimming in **Cenote Dzitnup ★★★** near Valladolid is thrilling, and almost always promises the company of local playmates.
- **Ojo de agua helechos**, El Corchito (*near Progreso*), has shallow swimming for kids.

Sailing and Cruising

- **Mangrove tour** at San Crisanto will reveal a hidden world.
- **Marina Silcer** in Chicxulub rents equipment for watersports, plus kite surfing training for kids!

Relax

- **Komchén de los Pájaros** in Dzemul near Mérida is a quiet retreat for the whole family to revel in the natural environment.

Shopping

- **El Taller Los Ceibos** in Muna near Uxmal demonstrates centuries old artesanal practices, and the kiln is sure to call the attention of children of all ages.

Advice for Parents

Bring plenty of non-toxic bug repellent for your child, no matter the time of year, and some for yourself as well! Also stock up on snacks, water and gasoline (if driving) wherever possible as service stations can be few and far between.

RELAX

The Yucatán may well be every escapists dream. Lush jungle and underground swimming holes make for easy disappearing acts. For those who seek personal rest and relaxation, the spas that are springing up all over the peninsula have a unique Mayan influence.

Quiet Spots and Nature

In the Yucatán, quiet is easy to find. These haunts are for those who like to stop, look and listen; from white sands and emerald waters that stretch as far as the eye can see, to lush jungle filled with bird-calls; or from ancient cities where you may well find yourself alone with a butterfly or an iguana, to haciendas whose silence echoes the changes of time,

- *See Beaches* for **San Felipe** and **Sisal**.
- *See Nature and Cenotes* for **Cenote Samula★★**.
- *See Mayan Cities* for **Aké**.
- *See Colonial Cities* for **Hacienda Yaxcopoil**.

Spas

Just 15 minutes north of Mérida, **El Spa de la Hacienda Xcanatun** (*www.xcanatun.com/spa/index.html*), has holistic and ancient Mayan treatments, while using modern techniques. This renovated hacienda is now an 18-room luxury hotel. Guests can have their massages in-room, and those who come for treatments only can opt for a bed in the abundant garden's *palapa*. The house specialty is a Mayan massage with honey and flowers. The calming aloe wrap will send you to another time and place.

The award-winning **Yaxkin Spa at Hacienda Chichén Resort**, (*www.haciendachichen.com/spa-maya-retreat.htm*) bases its treatments in the wisdom of ancient Mayan spiritual and ritual practices. Sacred natural essential elements such as *virgen* honey, *cacao*, aloe, herbs, flowers, and tropical fruits are employed with millennial skill, surrounded by the same jungle where they grow organically. Its director is a renowned *Ix-men*, or female healer. Treat yourself to warm raw sugar and *cacao* butter massage, meant to invigorate the energy flow in your body, and the gentle brushing of your skin and muscles with the finest chocolate and coconut oils.

The sophisticated **Coqui Coqui Day Spa** (*Calle de los Frailes, www.coquicoquispa.com*), in Valladolid, is just opening its doors to the public. It gives traditional massages, Reiki and reflexology, treatments for skin, hair and nails, and a botanical bath.

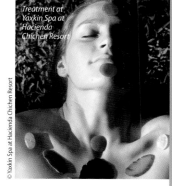

Treatment at Yaxkin Spa at Hacienda Chichén Resort

© Yaxkin Spa at Hacienda Chichén Resort

NIGHTLIFE

All-inclusive, all-nighter, all-you-can-drink clubs are a relative newcomer to the Yucatán, where a more traditional pace of life was once the norm. After Cancún, the biggest nightspot on the Riviera Maya is Playa del Carmen, while further west the best nightlife is found in Mérida. Outside of big tourist towns like Cancún and major cities like Mérida, there are scattered discos, nightclubs and "booze cruises", but not many. People enjoy strolling on the *Malecon* with a gentle breeze blowing through their hair, sitting out at a café and watching the world go by. There's everything to do, and nothing.

CANCÚN

Zona Hotelera – Many visitors come for Cancún's beaches and come to party. The nightlife scene has much more than just beach bars, with international DJs and acts regularly visiting the clubs here, while the Spring Break phenomenon brings in wave after wave of a young crowd looking to let their hair down. At this time of year the clubs are flooded, but the variety of nightlife ensures there is always somewhere else to go. Cancún's bars and nightclubs have re-invented themselves several times since the city first started to see mega resort and tourism traffic. The city's clubs grow more extravagant as the years go on, with some clubs, such as the **Coco Bongo**, presenting a multimedia frenzy of cover bands, gymnasts, fire breathers and sound and light shows. However, this young city's

nightlife scene is arguably still in its infancy, and tourism dollars will bring still more re-inventions. **Punta Cancún** is considered party central, with many of the places everyone knows, like Señor Frogs and the Hard Rock Cafe, while many venues cluster around **Forum by the Sea** (km9.5). In **El Centro**, the action centers on streets off **Avenida Tulum**. Taxis are eminently available in Cancún, but your hotel will probably provide a free or very cheap **bar tour**, taking guests in a bus or van to a different club each night, or even the top five clubs in one evening, depending on the hotel. Tours generally return to the hotel at 2am, but many hotel bars stay open until 4am, while others are open to guests 24/7. 10pm–1am is peak time in Cancún nightlife; leaving the die-hards to party on.

Bars

The cheaper brethren of the expensive clubs, bars are found by the bucketload in Cancún. From Corona Bar to La Madonna, they usually provide food day and night; in the evening the emphasis changes to drinking, dancing and entertainment.

Bars usually close around 1am. Charges are normally per drink,

---

Dancing in the Streets

There is plenty of fun to be had outdoors in Cancún outside of the beach bars. Dancers and mariachi bands are found on numerous street corners in both the Zona Hotelera and El Centro. Party Center courtyard is a hotspot for traditional Mexican music.

MUST DO

but open bar deals are common with prices usually between $20–$30 for a few hours (Señor Frogs is closer to $40).

Bling

Blvd. Kukulcán, Km13.5. 9pm–4am. 998-840-6014.

With an outdoor terrace overlooking the lagoon, this chic bar attracts a 30-something crowd with its top spec sound system, cocktails and sushi and sashimi bar.

Carlos N Charlie's

Blvd. Kukulcán Km. 5.5. No cover charge. 998-849-4053. www.carlosandcharlies.com.

This bar-restaurant is open for lunch and dinner. Sassy waiters are as likely to get you up to join a conga line as they are to take your order. Live rock, Latin and pop music starts around 9pm.

Corona Bar

Zona Hotelera, Blvd. Kukulcán Km9. 998-883-2145.

Corona Beer is king at this casual bar in the heart of the hotel zone, just in front of **The City** nightclub. There is no cover charge, making it popular with folks looking for somewhere to start the evening before heading off to one of the big clubs nearby.

Dady Rock Bar & Grill

Blvd. Kukulcán, Km9.5, next door to Dady'o's. Cover $16; $35 with open bar. 6pm–late. 998-883-1626. www.dadyrock.com.mx.

The sister bar of the Dady 'O super club, Dady Rock's '**Terrasta**'

Best of the Rest
Looking for an easy bar crawl? Try the **Bar Hopper Tour** (*$65 for 7 hours at 3 bars*), which meets at 9pm at **CoCo Bongo**, 10:45 at Señor Frogs and 11:45pm at The City, Cancún's biggest club.

opens at 6pm (playing reggae, hip hop, R&B and reggaeton), while the rest of the bar opens at 8pm. Live bands and DJs keep dancers going on the floor while the MC, contests and shows keep the atmosphere ramped up. Four bars spread over two levels.

Fat Tuesday

Zona Hotelera, Blvd. Kukulcán Km6.5. Cover $5. Pay per drink. 998-849-7199.

If you are after a raucous night of beer swilling then this is for you. Fat Tuesday has been MTV's Spring Break headquarters several times and is a firm favourite with students looking to party by the beach (bring towels and suntan lotion). A tradition in Cancún since 1992, Fat Tuesday (meaning Mardi Gras) serves huge daiquiris, holds bikini contests and parties noon until dawn. The club has a large indoor and outdoor area. As the crowds pack in it gets sweaty, so leave your best clothes at home and get ready for a beach party.

Hard Rock Café, Cancún

Forum by the Sea. 998–881-8120. www.hardrock.com

The Cancún outlet of this global chain has a multi-level 1950s style diner with a band stage and Rock 'n Roll memorabilia all over the walls. The Hard Rock is principally a place to eat during the day (American/Mexican), opening at 11am. Come the weekend, the live music ramps up and the joint is open until 2am (*Thu–Tue from 10:30pm*).

O Ultra Lounge

Blvd. Kukulcán Km9.5. 998-883-3333. www.oultralounge.com. No cover charge. Open Bar $28 (Dady 'O open bar valid here).

Between Dady'O and Dady Rock, O Ultra Lounge features European and American DJ dance music, a chill-out terrace and martinis.

Señor Frog's

Zona Hotelera, Blvd. Kukulcán Km9.5. Noon–3/4am. 998-883-1092. www.senorfrogs.com.

One of Cancún's most famous bars and a favorite with spring breakers, Señor Frogs is a mix between a water park, bar and fast food joint. By day the bar is more family

friendly, but at night it pulsates with music. As a club, Señor Frogs can accommodate 1,500 people, with DJs and live music daily, plus a karaoke bar open until 3am. The bar's water tube slide (not always open) dispatches guests into lagoon water of questionable cleanliness. Young university students get wild drunk, making this a consistently raucous venue.

La Madonna

La Isla, Blvd. Kukulcán Km12.5. 998-883-2222. www.lamadonna. com.mx. Noon–1am.

Fans of the martini should try this tony bar and restaurant set on the canal in La Isla shopping center. The bar has hundreds of martini cocktails, Italian cuisine and red leather chairs on a large patio.

La Taberna

El Centro, Av. Yaxchilan No. 23-A. 998-887-5423.

A casual sports bar/restaurant with internet access, events, competitions and table games. La Taberna has pool tables and almost every board game you can name. The bar runs a 24/7 two for one happy hour, while the restaurant serves American and Mexican food.

The Lobby Lounge

Ritz-Carlton Cancún. Retorno del Rey 36, off Blvd. Kukulcán Km13.5. 5pm–1am. 998-885-0808.

This refined nightspot has a terrace overlooking the lagoon, a selection of martinis and over 80 premium tequilas, as well as a sushi and seafood bar, humidor and live music Thu–Sun.

Clubs

Cancún's biggest clubs can accommodate thousands and have all-night entertainment from circus performances to bikini contests as the crowd dances to pounding music under a melee of balloons, lights, foam and ticker tape. Clubs usually charge between $35 and $40 for entry and an open bar. Open bar is usually available until 3am; thereafter you have to pay your own way. Expect long lines weekends and high season. Hotel clubs are generally more upscale, so dress to impress.

Azúcar

Dreams Cancún, Punta Cancún, Blvd. Kukulcán Km9. 998-848-7000. www.cancun-dreaming.com. Music 10pm–4am.

The biggest Latin music acts play at this refined club at the **Dreams Cancún** resort, making this the best Latin club in the city. Well-dressed locals cut impressive steps on the dance floor.

Cassis

Hyatt Cancún Caribe. Blvd. Kukulcán, Km10.5. 6pm–1am. 998-848-7800.

Live jazz played to a packed house, with renowned performers from around the country.

Christine

NH Krystal Cancún. Blvd. Kukulcán km9. 10pm–3am. No shorts or jeans. 998-883-1133.

Three bars and a large dance floor host pop classics from the 70s onward. Light show, strobes and foam parties.

 The City

Blvd. Kukulcán km. 9.5, (998) 848-8380. www.thecitycancun.com. Cover $30–$40 with open bar.

The City is Cancún's largest nightclub, a tri-level beast with laser shows, live music and capacity for over 4,000 people. Electronic and urban music are favorites here, with big name live acts visiting regularly, as well as top US and Mexican DJs.

During the day, the **Beach Club** opens at 10am with pool, wave machine (surfing and boogie boarding), waterslide, food, drinks and beach cabañas. Overlooking the boulevard is the **Terrace Bar**, while **The Lounge** has cocktails and downtempo music. At 10:30pm the club's nine bars and several VIP areas open to the hordes of dedicated partygoers. The City has its own team of 40 international-level **acrobats** producing shows nightly, including possibly the only eight-man bungee in the world. Circus-style **shows** here fly in time to the thumping music, but go far beyond mere fire juggling. The '**Russian Hammock**' group is seven lycra-clad acrobats who perform airborne somersaults and tricks off a trapeze, while the '**Pulsadas**' perform choreographed body-on-body balancing routines. In the '**Bungee**' act synchronized performers float, tumble and soar in time to the music in glowing costumes, while the '**Ladder**' act sees everyday work equipment turn into works of art. The '**Fabrics**' act involves aerial acrobatics performed high above the crowd on colorful flowing fabrics, tying themselves into intricate knots, poses, drops,

What to Watch for

• Cover charges vary between zero and $45, so planning ahead and shopping around is worthwhile. You can sometimes cut a deal with staff earlier in the evening when bars are more empty. On certain nights some bars and clubs waive cover charges for female guests.

• Tip waiters in table areas up front to guarantee good service. Open bar deals only work if your waiter takes orders!

• Shot girls roam clubs and bars selling tequila slammers and other hard spirits. For the uninitiated, too much tequila is definitely a bad thing. Shots are not covered by open bar deals ($2–$4 each).

• If paying per drink, try to pay each round; avoid bar tabs.

• As ever, keep an eye on your drinks at all times and don't accept drinks from strangers. Keep valuable within reach and don't leave cameras on tables.

and slides. The **Mastiles** (masts) act combines with big screen projections to give the sense that acrobats are jumping out of the screen, performing stunts while scaling and descending three masts set among the crowd. On hip-hop nights a team of **break dancers** heat up the crowd.

CoCo Bongo

Forum by the Sea, Blvd. Kulkulcán Km9.5. 10:30pm–3:30am. $40–$45 cover charge. 998-883-5061. www.cocobongo.com.mx.

There is no official dance floor at this world-renowned night club whose partially-clad international clientele dance on virtually any available surface. Popular with

Spring Break college kids, the 3,000 capacity club plays techno, salsa, house, Caribbean, 70s and 80s music. Shows include cover bands and impersonators of big acts like Queen, Robbie Williams, Madonna and Lou Bega (Mambo No5). Circus acts, dancers, trumpeters and drummers complement the acts. 'Beetlejuice' and 'The Mask' charge around the club dispensing tequila from the bottle as bubbles, balloons and ticker tape fall.
The stadium-style club has a main stage, central bar and three tiers of seating, with plenty of waiters keeping the drinks flowing. Tables are essential for those just here for the show (pre-reservation required). Arrive early to get a good spot as vantage points are scarce after 11pm. The show ends around 2am, but the dancing continues into the morning with 80s, 90s and Latin pop. Expect long queues on weekends and in high season.

Dady'O

Blvd. Kukulcán, Km9.5. 998-883-3333. www.dadyo.com.mx. Cover $20; $40 with open bar.

Cavernous Dady 'O has state-of-the-art lighting and sound, CO^2 effects, laser shows and top DJs. Six bars give easier access to the open bar service, while multiple levels of tables around the dance floor are attended by waiters.

Roots Jazz Club

El Centro, Calle Tulipanes 26, SM 22. 998-884 24 37. Open Tue–Sat 7pm–1am.

One of the best spots for live music downtown, with a sophisticated local clientele. Serves

Caribbean food to candle-lit tables. Shows usually start around 10pm, with music ranging from reggae to flamenco, jazz, and fusion.

Cultural Shows

The **National Folkloric Ballet of Mexico** (*Cancún Convention Center, Blvd. Kukulcán Km9; open bar; $48 dinner and show, $30 show only; cancuncenter.com; Toll free Mexico: 1-800-881-0400*) has traveled the world, visiting five continents and 30 countries, but its show is still performed week nights in Cancún. Drinks start at 6:30pm, dinner is at 7pm, followed at 8pm with an 80min performance by over 70 artists of traditional and modern dance, with locally-inspired music. **El Mexicano Restaurant** in the Costa Blanca Shopping Center has similar performances 7pm–11pm.

Dinner Cruises

Captain Hook Pirate Cruise

Departs 7pm from Playa Linda. $73/$37 kids (transport to/from hotel included in the ticket). www.capitanhook.com

El Galeon and El Bucancero are two replica 18C Spanish galleons (93ft) booze cruise ships. Up to 350 guests board each boat, which sails the bay with open bar, games, dancing and dinner. The ships converge and sword fights ensue as pirates swing aboard. The ships dock at 10:30pm. In 2008 a third ship was added to the fleet, crewed by characters from the Pirates of the Caribbean film. In quiet season, it is worth going on a Friday or Saturday night as only one ship sails when there are less guests.

Caribbean Carnaval

Playa Tortugas, km6.5. $85/$42 kids. 998-898-4312.

A true booze cruise, sailing a catamaran from Cancún to Isla Mujeres, with open bar and a buffet dinner at the 'El Pescador' beach club, with a Caribbean or Pirate Show, games, and prizes.

ISLA MUJERES

Smaller and more laid-back than Cancún, there is still plenty to do on Isla Mujeres, with plenty of beach bars (just look for the closest one) like **Buho's** on Playa Norte. Otherwise, most of the restaurants and bars are downtown. Many of these center on Avenue Hidalgo, such as **La Adelita** (*Av. Hidalgo Norte 12A*), a tequila bar, and **KoKo Nuts** (*Plaza Isla Mujeres*), which has live music. On Rueda Medina are **Jax Bar & Grill** (*on corner by north beach lighthouse*), which has live music until late, and **Pinguinos** (*in front of Hotel Posada del Mar*), open late for dancing. On Avenida Matamaros between Juárez and Hidalgo is **OM Bar** a mellow Moroccan-style place with beer on tap at each table. **Nitrox Club VIP** (*Av. Guerrero, off Av. Matamoros, Wed–Sun, 9pm–3am*) is the island's biggest club venue, playing Latin and dance music.

ISLA COZUMEL

Cozumel's nightlife centers around San Miguel, whose bars and cafés stretch along the waterfront over four or five blocks, with most of the action on Avenida Rafael Melgar. Evening entertainment is more family-friendly here than in Cancún. Sunday night is the big night out, when Cozumel's main square sees every generation turn out for music and dancing. Those familiar with Cancún's nightlife, Spring Break, and chain bars won't find many surprises here. **Carlos & Charlies** (*Av. Melgar 551*; **Señor Frogs** *disco upstairs*) is touristy and, like **Fat Tuesday** (*Av. Benito Juarez #2, north side of Plaza Central*), very similar to its Cancún sister bar (*see Cancún entries above*). Both of these are popular with the cruise ship crowd; the Punta Lagosta Pier is closest to town.

Cozumel has its own **Hard Rock Café** (*betw. Calle 2 Nte. & Juárez #2A, 10am–1am*), which has live bands in the evening. Other bars include **Kiss My Cactus** and **Viva Mexico** (*Av. Melgar; 10am–3am*). The latter is popular with locals and your best bet for late night partying to Latin music. Salsa fans should try **Café Salsa** (*Av. 10 betw B. Juarez and Calle 2*) for live music. More refined venues include **1.5 Tequila** (*Av. Melgar, corner of Calle 11 Sur*), a chic lounge bar serving cocktails and sushi with a fabulous view (go for sunset), and **Havana Club** (*Av. Melgar betw Calle 6 & Calle 8*), an upstairs cigar bar that has live jazz most evenings. The island's main disco is the **Neptuno** (*Rafael Melgar at Calle 11 Sur*).

PLAYA DEL CARMEN

Similar to Cancún, but more stylish, Playa is also a better option than nearby Cozumel for those really looking to party. Venues here import top DJs from around the world, while the town's hippy past lives on in its unpretentious rock and reggae bars, and

Mamitas beach parties.

Quinta Avenida (5th) is the town's activity hub. Many people take afternoon siestas and then head out for the night at 10pm to Playa's kicked back beach bars, live music venues, roof top lounges, sports bars and major nightclubs.

Alux

Pronounced 'Ah-loosh'. Revolution Av. about 5 blocks up from the 307.

Bar/restaurant/nightclub built inside a huge cenote (cave), with natural water and stalagmites. Thousands of colored lights shine among the stalactites. Unique doesn't begin to describe it.

Bali

Calle12 Norte, 5th Av. and 10th Av. Open 10pm. www.baliclub.com.mx. 984-803-2864.

The closest thing Playa has to a Cancún megaclub is this Bali-style 1,200 capacity behemoth with high-tech light shows, fire and water effects, acts and all-nighters.

Blue Parrot

12th St. N and 1st Av. N. 984-873-0083. www.blueparrot.com.

A sandy Playa landmark, Blue Parrot DJs play chilled tunes during the day (*food 7.30am–6pm*). At nightfall the beach club features top international DJs in three different environments: Beach (*pop and retro, with fireshow at 11pm*), Palapa Lounge (*progressive dance*) and Sky Bar (*chill*) with views of the Caribbean and beachfront. Around the fence, the **Costa del Mar** bar is a nice place to chill out listening to reggae, while

Coco Maya parties until dawn to progressive dance music.

Deseo

5a Av. and Calle 12. 984-879-3620. www.hoteldeseo.com.

This South-Beach style boutique hotel (*see Must Stay*) has a rooftop bar with lounge beds surrounded by billowing curtains, old silent movies projected on the wall and various lounge music spun by DJs.

La Santanera

Calle 12 Norte, between Av. 5 and Av. 10. 8pm–6am.

A dynamic and very Mexican club with an incredible sound system, Latin music, an air conditioned chill out area, and an upstairs terrace perfect for people watching.

Om Lounge

Av. 1 bis, corner of Calle 12 Norte. 984-879-4784. www.omplaya.com.

A chilled cocktail bar with mixed Near East and Asian decor. Nearby competitor **Kartabar** has a Middle-Eastern theme, hookah pipes, divans and belly dancers.

Xcaret

Xcaret has a pair of **theatres** capable of seating 6,000 and puts on colorful, complex shows featuring live music, acrobats and dancers. Go and spend the day in the park then stay for dinner and the show.

Tulum

Most of the party action in Tulum is on Fri and Sat nights at the cabañas on the beach. **Mezzanine** (*Beach Rd, km1.5, 8am–11pm, 998-112-2845, www.mezzanine.com. mx*) is a boutique hotel that hosts Ibiza-style **beach parties** (**Fiesta en La Playa**) on Fridays with occasional big name international DJs spinning the latest house 9pm–2am. **La Zebra** further on at km8.5 has salsa parties on Sundays and gives salsa lessons.
Habana Café (*Av. Tulum, between Jupiter and Acuario*) has two bars, rooftop dancing, live music and DJs on weekends.

MÉRIDA
The city streets come alive at night with locals and tourists out in the bars, restaurants, parks, plazas and clubs. Evenings are all about people watching, and the Main Plaza is the best place for it. Saturday nights are called **Corazon de Mérida** (Heart of Mérida), when Calle 60 is closed to traffic from the plaza to Calle 55. Restaurants and bars put their tables and chairs out in the street and an open-air fiesta starts up with bands on every block, stilt walkers and other shows. Check newspapers for paid for shows and performances in the city on other nights.

There are several clubs in the downtown area frequented by tourists and locals, such as **El Cielo** (*Prolongación de Montejo; 7pm–3am*), a minimalist place popular on Thursdays and Fridays for its open bar. Don't even consider going to a Mérida nightclub before 11pm; many keep going until 5–7am. **Tequila Rock** (*Prolongacion Montejo and Av. Campestre*), **Mambo Café** (*Plaza Las Americanas Shopping Mall*) and **Tequila Bongo** (*Plaza Dorada Shopping Mall*) are other popular discos.

NIGHTLIFE

RESORTS

Resort hotels abound on the Yucatán's Caribbean coast, from the mega resorts of Cancún to adults-only boutiques and new 'eco-resorts'. Many of these hotels offer all-inclusive packages, which is reflected in the price. *For price ranges, see the legend on the following pages under 'Hotels'.*

CANCÚN

Zona Hotelera

Hilton Cancún Golf and Spa Resort $$-$$$

Blvd. Kukulcán, Km17.5. 998-881-8000. www1.hilton.com.

446 luxury accommodations on a large white sand beach, with a spa and an 18 hole par 72 golf course meandering through Mayan ruins, mangroves and jungle.
The family package includes children's activities.

🐬 Dreams Cancún Resort & Spa $$$

Punta Cancún, 998-848-7000. Toll-free: 866-2DREAMS. www.dreamsresorts.com.

This luxurious, 376 room, all-inclusive resort with Mayan-inspired architecture has an incredible number of activities for everyone in the family. Set on a long, quiet beach, guests can watch the dolphin swim program, run by 🐬**Delphinus**, from the balcony of many of the rooms. A lively but not raucous property where, on the way to your room, you get a feel for Mexican culture as you walk past displays of crafts and jewelry for sale. There's a first class spa, two pools, a health club, and a few small Mayan ruins on property. The excellent restaurants serve food a cut above that found in other all-inclusives. They include an extensive buffet at **World Café**, **Oceana** seafood restaurant, and specialty dining at **Himitsu**, a top Japanese spot with private tables on the beach, surrounded by fire-lit torches. Several snack bars are open for a quick lunch or snack during daytime hours, and there are multiple bars throughout the property. Guests receive 20% off at

Ritz Carlton Cancún

©The Ritz Carlton Cancún

Paloma Bonita, one of Cancún's top restaurants (not included in all inclusive programs). **Azúcar** nightclub, another popular Cancún landmark gives free admission and two complimentary drinks to resort guests.

Fiesta Americana Grand Coral Beach $$$

Blvd. Kukulcán Km9.5.
998-881-3200.
www.fiestamericana.com.

602 suites on 11 floors have sweeping views of the Caribbean. Five restaurants, four bars and a complimentary Fiesta Kids Club hosting children 4–12 with daytime supervision, activities, and meals. The meeting and function space (7,900sq m/85,000sq ft) can accommodate up to 1,800.

Gran Meliá Cancún $$$

Blvd. Kukulcán, Km16.5. 998-193-0090. www.gran-melia.com.

This resort received the AAA four diamond award for 2007, and Leading Spa of the World award. It features four pools and has activity programs for children and adults, with a nine hole, par three golf course, tennis courts, and two paddle tennis courts.

CasaMagna Marriott Cancún Resort $$-$$$$

Blvd. Kukulcán,
Retorno Chac L-41. 998-881-2000.
www.casamagnacancun.com.

The CasaMagna was completely renovated after Hurricane Wilma and now has 418 rooms and 34 suites, each with a private balcony. The hotel has 3 restaurants—a steakhouse, Japanese restaurant, and bar. Resort facilities include an outdoor children's pool, tennis, volleyball, and a fitness center with saunas. Easy access to nearby scuba diving and snorkeling and plenty of outdoor activities.

Le Méridién Cancún Resort & Spa $$-$$$$

Km14, Retorno Del Rey, Lote 37-1.
998-881-2200. www.starwood
hotels.com/lemeridien.

The 213 residential-style, private balconied guest rooms have Caribbean views. The spacious 1,400sq m/15,000sq ft European-style Spa del Mar has an extensive menu of premier skin and body treatments.

Westin Resort & Spa Cancún $$-$$$$

Blvd. Kukulcán, Km20, Zona Hotelera. 998-848-7400. www. starwoodhotels.com/westin.

Near the Nichupté Lagoon, at the quiet end of the Hotel Zone, the resort includes "private" beaches and four pools, the Heavenly Spa, countless water sports, tennis, golf, and a gym. The 379 guest rooms feature contemporary décor and Caribbean or lagoon views.

JW Marriott Cancún Resort $$$-$$$$

Blvd. Kukulcán, Km14.5, Lote 40-A.
998-848-9600; 888-813-2776.
www.marriott.com.

The 448-room property has a connected pathway to the adjacent Marriott CasaMagna. Amenities include 2 outdoor pools, plus children's outdoor pool, tennis, a dive pool with artificial reef, spa, and fitness center with classes. The well-respected Marriott Kids' Club has arts and crafts and rainy day activities. Nearby water sports options include scuba diving, snorkeling, and water-skiing.

Ritz Carlton Cancún $$$$

Retorno del Rey #36. 998-881-0808. www.ritzcarlton.com.

With a culinary center, the luxurious Kayantá Spa, a Cliff Drysdale Tennis Center and award winning restaurants, guests will never want to leave.

ISLA MUJERES

Excellence
Playa Mujeres $$$$

Prolongación Bonampak, S/N, Punta Sam Lote Terrenos 001 MZ. 001 Sm. 003, Zn. Continental de Isla Mujeres. Toll-free: 866-540-2585. www.excellence-resorts.com.

Playa Mujeres is the newest luxury resort destination in the region. It covers a secluded, untouched, 20mi long peninsula only 25min north of Cancún. The Excellence Playa Mujeres, adults-only resort takes over two miles of powdery white sand. The community includes an inland marina, spa, and Greg Norman signature golf course right on the Caribbean.

COZUMEL

Wyndham
Cozumel Resort & Spa $$

Carr. Costera Sur. Km12.9. US Toll-free: 1-888-293-0293. www.wyndhamcozumel.com.

A unique all-inclusive resort that's ideal for families, groups, divers, and golfers, and also includes a "child-free" adults-only section, "Sabor". Over 312 rooms on 609m/2,000ft of white sand beach, the wide variety of recreational facilities and activities includes: three swimming pools, lighted tennis and multipurpose courts, fitness center, and non-motorized water sports including hobie cats, kayaks, snorkel equipment and windsurfing. For the younger set, a supervised kids program provides daily activities and theme parties, nightly live entertainment and shows at the indoor theater, plus a private pier, teen's club and soda bar for smoothies.

Coral Princess
Hotel & Resort $$$

Carr. Costera Nte Km. 2.5. 987-872-3200; US Toll-free: 1-800-253-2702. www.coralprincess.com.

Remodeled resort with 136 rooms, gym, free internet, terrace restaurant, lobby bar, karaoke, pool table and flat screen TVs.

El Cid La Ceiba
Beach Hotel $$$

Carr. Chankanaab, Km. 4.5. 987-872-0844, US Toll-free: 1-800-435-3240. www.elcid.com.

Newly renovated, long-time Cozumel favorite. Excellent scuba diving right from beach with a famous airplane wreck in shallow water. 107sq m/1,150sq ft fitness center, spa with unique Mayan and Temazcal treatments, kids playground and pool. Excellent snorkeling, onsite: Babieca Dive Center (*see Meso-American Reef*).

Melià Cozumel $$$

*Carr. Costera Nte Km5.8.
987-872-9870; US Toll-free: 1-800-
336-3542. www.solmelia.com.*

148 rooms, including 59 suites,
free Wi-Fi in public areas, two outdoor pools, two lit tennis courts,
daytime entertainment programs,
spa, Flintstones Land (ages 4–12),
three restaurants, a snack bar and
five bars.

Aura Cozumel
Wyndham Grand Bay $$$$

*Carr. Costera sur Km.12.9. 987-872-
9320, US/CAN Toll-free: 866-551-
aura. www.auraresorts.com.*

An ultra-superior standard adults-
only resort where all 87 suites
feature an ocean view balcony,
flat screen high definition TV,
Wi-Fi internet access, iPod dock
with radio alarm clock, electronic
laptop-sized safe deposit box, 300
thread Egyptian cotton bed linen
and Comfortline beds. Some of
the suites are "swim-up". Facilities
include two restaurants, three bars,
a solarium, three outdoor Jacuzzis,
a water mirror with relaxation
pool, lazy river leading into a pool,
fitness center, and direct access to
the Islander Spa in the Wyndham
Cozumel Resort and Spa complex.

Iberostar
Cozumel Hotel $$$$

*Carr. Costera Sur Km. 17.782,
Paraiso El Cedral. 987-872-9900.
www.iberostar.com.*

An all-inclusive with romantic
thatched roof bungalows scattered among lush foliage enclos-
ing 306 rooms. There is a buffet
restaurant plus three specialty res-

taurants (reservations guaranteed
twice per week). The renovated
spa has a wide selection of massage and beauty treatments. The
wide variety of entertainment
and daily activities include sports,
competitions, games, and shows
in the evening (Lucy´s Mini-Club is
for ages 4–12).

Park Royal Cozumel,
Playa Paraiso $$$$

*Km3.5 Carr. a Chankanaab.
987-872-0700.
www.park-royalhotels.com.*

An all-inclusive resort with a
beautiful central space filled with
swimming pools, flowing water
and greenery tying the buildings
together. The spacious open lobby
seems to be cut from the rocks.
A kids' club keeps children busy
and has its own waterslide pool, in
addition to the other three pools.
Beach access is only through an
underpass from the resort, making
it very private. Beautifully laid out
with different areas for sunning,
two Jacuzzis, a bar, snack bar,
and a wooden platform over the
water for yoga. **AquaWorld** dive
and watersports shop onsite (*see
Meso-American Reef*). Evening
entertainment ranges from bingo
in the lobby to performances in
the large open-air theater.

Presidente
InterContinental $$$$

*Carr. a Chankanaab, Km6.5. 987-
872-9500; US Toll free 1-800-327-
0200. www.intercontinental.com.
220 Rooms and suites.*

The Presidente lives up to all the
awards it has won, creating an
atmosphere of charm, calm and

grace on a beautifully laid out half mile of white sand beach with a large swimming pool reflecting turquoise water. Divers and snorkelers love the onsite scuba center. The Chiqui Club takes care of kids all day, and the fabulous 🏊 **Mandara spa** is one of the best in the world (*see Must Relax*). The Presidente decorates its rooms with the most unusual and diverse assortment of animals made from towels that you'll ever see.

The hotel built a special "iguana condo" to house the local iguanas, rather than chasing them off.

PUERTO MORELOS

Hotel Marina El Cid Spa & Beach Resort $$$

Blvd. El Cid Unidad 15. 998-872-8999; US Toll-free: 866-823-0099. www.elcid.com

A welcoming retreat tucked away from crowded downtown Cancún hotel rooms. Spacious garden or ocean view junior to three-bedroom suites. Intimate design and warm Mexican hospitality give the feeling of being at home, yet pampered.

Ceiba del Mar Hotel & Spa $$$$$

Costera Nte Lote 1 SM 10 Mza. 998-872-8063; US Toll-free: 877-545-6221, MX 01-800-426-9772. www.ceibadelmar.com.

A cocktail welcomes you to this luxury hotel that mixes Mayan and Mexican architecture in its 45 rooms, 36 master suites and seven penthouses with breathtaking views. 300 thread-count cotton sheets, free Wi-Fi, private balconies or terraces (with hammock), entertainment systems, soft bath robes and twice daily housekeeping. The two restaurants serve Yucatecán food, plus grilled and wood-fired oven specialties. The spa has a sauna, steam room, Swiss shower, plunge pool, whirlpool and gym.

🏊 Mayakoba $$$$$

Carr. 307 Km298, Playa del Carmen Solidaridad. 984-206-3000. www.fairmont.com/mayakoba.

An interconnected group of luxury resorts, spear-headed by the **Fairmont Mayakoba**. The Fairmont is luxury personified with 401 elegant rooms scattered among the main building and villas spread through the indigenous jungle, with 34 beach and lagoon casitas—each with a memorable view. The property is home to the Willow Stream Spa (*see Must Relax*) and was awarded five AAA diamonds in 2006.

The **Rosewood Mayakoba** (*984-875-8000*) has 120 suites and a spa (*see Must Relax*), while minimalist **Viceroy** and Asian-style **Banyan Tree** will open in 2009. Within this large complex's grounds is the 🏌️ **El Camaléon** golf course, designed by Greg Norman, and host of the first PGA tournament in Mexico (Feb 2007); The Mayakoba Classic.

PLAYA DEL CARMEN

Royal Hideaway Playacar $$$$

Lote Hotelero #6 Fracc., Playacar. 984-873-4500. www.royalhideaway.com.

All-inclusive and adults only with 200 rooms in Mexican colonial style and two- to three-floor villas.

Mandarin Oriental Riviera Maya $$$$$

Carr. 307 Km298.8. 984-877-3888. www.mandarinoriental.com/ rivieramaya.

Pure luxury set amidst 36 acres of tropical forests with views over the Caribbean Sea, lagoons and a freshwater lake. Guests are escorted to rooms by golf cart along winding paths and waterways, arriving at private villas. Rooms feature rainforest showers, outdoor stone bathtubs and white courtyards. The hotel also has spa rooms, beachfront *casitas* with private pools and the 2,600sq ft Presidential Villa (with personal butler and chef). The Little Fans club accommodates children (aged 4–12), while adults choose from seven bars and restaurants.

Hacienda Trés Ríos $$$$$

Carr. Cancún-Tulum, Km. 54. 998-891-5263; USToll-free: 800-224-4231. www.haciendatresrios.com.

The first of three hotels on this extensive site opens July 2009. Nestled in a natural reserve with mangrove forests, ten clear cenotes, and a mile of virgin beaches. Part of the property will be left untouched as a private reserve.

PUERTO AVENTURAS

Omni Puerto Aventuras Hotel Beach Resort $$$

Carr. 307 Km269. 984-875-1950. www.omnihotels.com.

An intimate, 30-room resort with private jacuzzi on each balcony or patio, set in a yachting community of villas and luxury condominiums. Puerto Aventuras was the first "planned" community in the Yucatán, and was built using native materials. Coral reef just offshore provides excellent snorkeling (*see Meso-American Reef*).

TULUM

EcoTulum Resorts & Spa $$

Cabañas Copal, Azulik, Zahra. Carr. Tulum Ruinas Km. 5, Rojo Gomez rumbo a Punta Allen. 54-115-918-6400; US/Can Toll-free: 888-898-9922. www.ecotulum.com.

Three holistic resorts share this property. **Cabañas Copal** is a seaside holistic spa resort that gets you off the beaten path for a truly alternative vacation experience in a rustic, candlelit eco-hotel, away from telephones and electricity. The two small sister resorts, **Azulik** and **Zahra**, have electicity and other amenities.

Dreams Tulum Resort & Spa $$$$

Km23 Tulum, between Playa and Tulum, 75min south.

One of the best all-inclusives, with a beautiful, secluded beach and activities for everyone (also perfect for honeymooners). A wonderful 433 room property designed for privacy. One of the best spas (*www.DreamsTulumResortSpa.com*) in the Yucatán uses traditional Mayan bath ritual. Have an analysis first to determine recommended treatments. Superb gourmet restaurants.

HOTELS

Accommodations in the Yucatán run the gamut from villas in sprawling luxury developments to a basic budget room with a bath down the hall. History, culture, design and often pure location imbue the very best of these hotels with a true sense of place. Accommodations range from **all-inclusive resorts** (usually in the higher price range) to **luxury hotels** in prime areas, **haciendas** in areas influenced by the Spanish occupation, **cabañas** on beaches, **mid-range** and **budget** hotels in the cities and small towns, and **guesthouses** and **B&Bs**. Resorts (*see the Resorts section for our top picks*) are divided between **couples-only** and **family**. The latest trend is a combination—a large family-friendly resort with a section set aside for couples only.

Cities – Around Mérida and the colonial cities there are more guesthouses and renovated haciendas, while beachtowns like Cancún have the mega-resorts and luxury beachfront properties. Among the tourism monoliths of the coastline, a few small, beachfront hotels still hold their ground.

Islands – Isla Mujeres has a good selection of quaint properties, particularly on the north shore and downtown, but a growing number of super-luxury resorts are being built on the west and southwest. Isla Cozumel is in a similar situation, with a greater mix of smaller, more intimate and less expensive lodgings still available amid the larger hotels and resorts.

Caribbean Coast – On the mainland, the Riviera Maya has a multitude of higher priced properties and resorts with golf courses and extensive facilities. Moving south into the Costa Maya, the area is much less developed and you'll find small hotels with fewer amenities, little hidden gems built in traditional Mayan fashion on secluded beaches, and more of an ecological focus.

Inland – You will find every type of hotel under the sun here, but look out for haciendas near the old colonial cities, as well as for eco-tourism lodges. More and more of the latter appear every year.

Specialist Resorts – Specialized activity resorts are becoming more common on the Caribbean coastline, taking advantage of the spectacular underwater reef system, cenotes, lagoons, and beautiful bays. Some properties cater to ecotourists, others to scuba divers or the fishing crowd.

Mega Resorts – Looking for an all-inclusive holiday? See Resorts.

Shopping Havens – For visitors who prefer shopping above all other activities, many hotels in Cancún are part of, or close to a big shopping mall.

Haciendas – Spanish colonization, especially in Mérida and the west, left a number of evocative haciendas that have been turned into beautiful historic hotels. The budget and mid-range places will be found in isolated locations and in the bigger city centers and they often take advantage of local materials and decorate in the Mexican style.

Booking – Most of the properties in this list can be booked online; if not through their own websites, then through a travel or hotel booking site. Be sure to check the internet for "web-only" discounts. In general, the high-end properties are located in the tourist centers—Cancún, Cozumel, the Riviera Maya, and Mérida. Yet there are many more choices far from the maddening crowds.

$	<$100
$$	$100–$175
$$$	$175–$250
$$$$	$250–350
$$$$$	>$350

CANCÚN

Zona Hotelera
See Resorts.

El Centro
Downtown Cancún has a good selection of low–mid-range lodgings as it caters to business travelers rather than free-spending tourists.

$ Cancún Inn Suites

El Patio, Av. Bonampak # 51, (across street from Puerto Cancún towers) Supermanzana 2A. 998-884-3500. www.Cancún-suites.com

Charming 18 room inn with an 'old hacienda' atmosphere. Beautiful colonial courtyard. Very secure, two blocks from main downtown tourist district.

$ Hotel Batab

Av. Chichén Itzá No. 52, SM 23. 998-884-3822. US Toll-free: 888-835-4121. www.hotelbatab.com.

Traditional hospitality in a small property with 68 A/C rooms and onsite restaurant open

7am–10pm. Has meeting facilities for 120, wireless internet in common areas, baby sitting arranged by front desk. A few blocks from the bus station and close to crafts markets and restaurants.

$ Rey del Caribe

Ave. Uxmal at Náder, Ciudad Cancún. 998-884-2028. www.reycaribe.com. 25 rooms.

What's not to like about this little eco-gem in the heart of expensive Cancún? Rooms are comfy, the cafe is great, and the composting and solar-power energy leave a respectably small carbon footprint. Kitchenettes seal the deal.

$ Suites Villa Italia

Av. Bonampak, Manzana 10, Lote 52-53 Supermanzana 4. 892-4261. www.suitesvillaitalia.com.

Adults-only hotel (*children 15+*) in a convenient location, steps from Plaza Las Americas mall, one block from Avenida Tulum. 16 contemporary Italian-designed suites with fully-equipped kitchens, living and dining room area and daily in-room continental breakfast.

$-$$ Terracaribe Hotel

Av. Lopez Portillo #70, corner Av. Bonampak. 998-880-0448. www.terracaribe.com.

Standard downtown hotel with amenities of a more expensive lodging. Remodeled pool, children's pool, sun deck, Jacuzzi, plus Solarium Terrace with massage area (8am–7pm). Has a beach club, plus free transportation to the club and hotel zone 9am–5pm.

Isla Mujeres

$ Villas Punta Sur

Carr. a Garrafón Km6. 998-877-0572. www.villaspuntasur.com.

Six furnished one and two bedroom apartments with private entrance terrace, no phone or TV. Upstairs apartments have an ocean view while downstairs ones have garden view. The property is surrounded by peaceful gardens, with a palapa and hammocks.

 $$ Avalon Reef Club

Calle Zazil Ha s/n Int 7 Islote Yunque. US Toll-free: 888-774-0040. www.avalonreefclub.com.

This unique, all-inclusive resort is a private islet sanctuary set on a sugar-white sand beach (accessible only by ferry). Private villas are built directly along rocky coastline across the pier and away from main property (perfect for families). The hotel has a kids' pool, spa and fitness center, snorkeling park, on-site scuba facilities, natural pool, two restaurants, two bars, access to golf facilities, a kids program and a "stay at one play at three" program applicable to **Avalon Baccara Cancún** and **Avalon Grand Cancún**.

$$ Casa Sirena

Av. Hidalgo between Bravo and Allende. www.sirena.com.mx.

An historic Spanish colonial-style residence and boutique hotel. The quiet neighborhood is a 10min walk to beaches, restaurants and shopping. Includes gourmet Mexican breakfast, as well as cocktails at sunset.

$$$ na Balam

Calle Zazil-Ha 118. 998-877-0279. www.nabalam.com.

31 rooms and suites here are minimalist but cozy, with no TV or phone. The hotel provides massage and yoga classes for relaxation. Zazil ha Restaurant, overlooking the beach, features Mayan, fusion, and vegetarian cuisine.

$$$$ Casa De Los Sueños

Carr. a Garrafón, Fracc. Turqueza lote 9 A y B. 998-877-0651. www.casadelossuenosresort.com.

A peaceful environment pervades this luxury ten room boutique hotel with no televisions, telephones, alarm clocks, or guests under-21. The ALMAR Lounge and Spa Zenter are also on property.

$$$$ Villa Rolandi Hotel

Fracc. Laguna Mar SM. 7 Mza. 75 Lotes 15 y 16, Carr. Sac-Bajo. 998-999-2000. www.villarolandi.com.

Swiss-owned Villa Rolandi lies between the beach and Laguna Makax. The hotel's 35 accommodations fall into four categories—20 junior suites, eleven deluxe junior suites, three standard oceanview rooms and one presidential suite. The Casa Rolandi Restaurant draws local gourmets, while the spa provides Thalasso Therapy.

COZUMEL
(see Resorts)

$ Villa Maya

Carr. Transversal to San Gervasio turnoff. 987-872-1750.

Cozumel Dive Resorts – Small, dedicated dive resorts.

Scuba Club Cozumel –
*Av. R Melgar Prol s, Km1.5.
987-872-1800.* A beachfront
hacienda-style hotel one mile
from town. Pool, restaurant,
scuba diving, snorkeling, boating, beach and air con.
Caribe Blu *(formerly Hotel
Lorena) Carr. Costa Sur Km2.2.
987-872-0188.* A 22 room,
moderately priced hotel for
divers. Friendly staff, intimate
atmosphere. Every room is
air-conditioned with cable TV
and an ocean view with private
balcony or patio area. Connected with Blue Angel Dive
Shop. Restaurant and bar.
Hotel Fontán – *Carr. Playa San
Juan Km2.5, Northern Hotel Zone.
987-872-0300. www.hotels
fontan.com.* 46 room mod-
erately priced dive resort, 10
minutes from town. Northern
location means a long boat ride
to the best dive sites.

Truly an eco-adventure away from
it all. Three traditional Mayan *ripios*
(thatched oval-shaped wooden
cabañas with two doorways) are
in a partly cleared area of jungle
close to the San Gervasio ruins.
Temazcal spa on property. Has hot
running water, biking, hiking and
fabulous bird watching.

$$ Ventanas al Mar

*Domicilio conocido, east side
of island. 987-105-2684.
www.ventanasalmar.com.mx.*

Next door to **Coconuts Res-
taurant** (**$$**), this is the only
accommodation on the windward
east coast. The ecolodge has 16
rooms featuring kitchenettes with
microwave, and no phones or
TVs. Bring provisions to stock your
kitchenette.

$$ Villas Las Anclas

*325 South 5th Av. 987-872-5476.
www.lasanclas.com.*

Small, quiet, intimate hotel, with
two-story suites. One block from
Dive Pier and 1.5 blocks from main
plaza. Daily maid service, abundant
purified water and fresh ground
coffee provided. Complimentary
wireless internet.

$$–$$$ Playa Azul
Golf & Beach Resort

*Costera Norte Km4, Zona
Hotelera Norte. 987-872-0043.
www.playa-azul.com.*

Great for golfers, Playa Azul includes greens fees at the Cozumel
Country Club golf course (5min
away) in its room rates. All 51
rooms and suites have balconies,
some facing the beach. American
breakfast is included, and the hotel
provides moped and car rentals,
free internet and a billiards table.

RIVIERA MAYA
(see Resorts)

$ Casa Willis

*Paamul. 984-133-5992.
www.scubamex.com/casawil.html.*

Exclusively for divers, oceanfront,
fully furnished Casa Willis has four
air-conditioned rental accom-

modations on its first and third floors. The three units are like small apartments, with satellite TV and wireless internet. Just walk down the beach to Scuba Mex dive shop.

$ Moongate Hotel

5A Av. Norte esq Calle 14 bis, Playa del Carmen. www.tukanhotels.com.

The beach is one street away from the Caribbean-style Moongate on Fifth Avenue. Sister hotel, **El Tukan**, is very close, with two charming restaurants: Los Tulipanes and Living Bar.

$ Villa Cobá

Carr. Tulúm Novo Xcan Km. 42, Cobá. 984-206-7001. www.villasarqueologicas.com.mx.

Villa Cobá overlooks a serene lake, close to the small community of Cobá and a ten-minute walk to the ancient Mayan ruins. 43 guestrooms, pool and patio. Lush tropical foliage gives a feeling of seclusion.

$$ Ana y José Hotel and Spa

Carr. 307, Km7, Bocapaila Tulum. 998-880-5629. www.anayjose.com.

Blends the tranquility of a fishermen's village with the features of a top level 21-room resort on an empty beach. The restaurant features Mayan cuisine delicacies with Dona Ana's 25-year tradition.

$$$ Deseo

5a Avenida at Calle 12, Playa del Carmen. 984-879-3620; 866-978-0891. www.hoteldeseo.com.

Chic, understated comfort in a hip, adults-only lodging in the center of Playa's happening hotel and restaurant zone. Rooms have internet connection and music; the property has a lounge, Jacuzzi, and plenty of attitude.

$$$ Hidden Beach Au Naturale Club

Km95 Carr. 307, Tulum. 984-875-7000. www.lifestyles-resorts.com.

Adults only, clothing optional resort in Kantenah Bay, an hour south of Cancún; 42 ocean-front suites in two two-story buildings. Unique beachfront swimming pool with a lazy river and huge beachfront hot tub. Intimate, secluded hideaway for naturist travelers and discrete lifestylers.

$$$$ Hotel Esencia

Carr. 307, 20min from Playa. 984-873-4835; US Toll-free: 877-528-3490, www.hotelescencia.com.

A 50-acre private estate, once the retreat of an Italian duchess, with breathtaking beachfront, two swimming pools, day spa, gourmet restaurant, and an indulgent atmosphere.

$$$$ Paraiso de la Bonita

Carr. 307, Km328, SM 31, Bahía Petempich, 10min from Puerto Morelos. 998-872-8300. www.paraisodelabonita.com.

This intimate, Mayan-style boutique resort is furnished with antiques. It boasts private-terraced suites spread over 14 acres of landscaped gardens and mangroves on a long beach. Each suite has a private terrace overlooking the ocean. There is fine dining in a variety of restaurants, a 24,000sq ft spa, plus a 48ft catamaran for hire.

COSTA MAYA

$ Balamku

Carr. Mahahual Km5.7. 983-838-0083, www.balamku.com.

Six elegant cabañas with fans, hot and cold running water, room service and internet on a private, secluded beach built with respect for the environment. Activities include snorkeling and scuba diving on the local reef or at Chinchorro Banks; kayaking; fishing; visiting Mayan ruins; and relaxing in the unspoiled beauty of nature.

$ Beach Garden Hotel B&B

N Carr. Costera Río Indio-Uvero Km20.5, Mahahual. www.mayan beachgarden.com.

This secluded hotel is set on spectacular Placer beach, 20km/12.4mi north of Mahahual and the Costa Maya Pier. Solar powered cabañas have private decks, hammock, hot showers and a sandy swimming beach. Excellent snorkeling and diving, close to Biosfera Sian Ka'an. Spa services, bar, restaurant.

 $ Costa De Cocos

Hwy. 307 to sign for Mahuahual, turn right at road to Xcalak, US Toll-free: 800-538-6802. www.costadecocos.com.

This remote outpost is in a jungle habitat filled with birds. Chinchorro Banks are off-shore, but reefs off property are great. Take a skiff to San Pedro Town, Ambergris Caye or Belize. Flyfish Costa de Cocos,

Caribbean flats and Chetumal Bay for bonefish, permit and tarpon.

 $ Dreamtime Dive Resort

Mahahual Coast Rd. Km2.5, Mahahual. 983-834-5823; US Tel: 904-730-4337. www.dreamtimediving.com.

A true eco-resort (accommodations closed for redevelopment—currently provided by nearby partner hotels) with authentic solar and wind-powered Mayan cabañas with hot showers. The beach is pristine, while reefs and Chinchorro Banks are in easy reach. Modern amenities include high-speed wireless internet.

$ La Posada De Los 40 Cañones

Km1.5 Mahahual Av., past Limones. 983-123-8591. www.los40canones.com.

On main street in the center of town, La Posada is named for a local shipwreck (good dive site). There are four superior rooms (with A/C), four standard (no AC), and two suites. The onsite Italian restaurant cooks pasta and fresh fish. Just across the street is 40 Cannon's beach club.

$ Posada Pachamama

Calle Huachinango s/n Col. Centro, Mahahual. 983-134-3049. www.posadapachamama.net.

Restaurant and six rooms with air con, Wi-Fi and hot water.

$$$ Las Ranitas

Carr. Tulum, Boca Paila Km9, Tulum. 984-877-8554. www.lasranitas.com.

Between the Sian Ka'an Biosphere Reserve and the archeological ruins of Tulum, this ecological nook is quiet and relaxing. Ten romantic beachside lodgings. Each day the cooks conjure up different dishes using fresh ingredients.

BAHÍA CHETUMAL

$$ Los Cocos

Av. Héroes 134, at Calle Chapultepec. 983-832-0544. www.hotelloscocos.com.

Modern, spacious rooms—some with balconies—complement this hotel's popular jungle-themed restaurant. Villas are available as is a pool, or stretch your legs with a short walk to the waterfront.

$$$ Rancho Encantado

Off Carr. 307, Km3. 983-831-0037. www.encantado.com.

This Mayan themed ranch has a numbers of small cottages overlooking Laguna Bacalar, 30min north of Chetumal. Swim and snorkel off the private dock.

RÍO BEC

$ Río Bec Dreams

Carr. 186, Escarcega-Chetumal Km142; 11km/6.8mi west of Xpuhil. 983-871-6057. www.riobecdreams.com.

Basic en-suite jungle cabañas with screened windows and terraces.

$$$ Explorean Kohunlich

Carr. Chetumal-Escarega Km5.65, same road as Kohunlich ruins. 877-397-5672. www.theexplorean.com.

An ecological resort on the outskirts of Kohunlich, with private, luxurious Mexican-style suites strung along a jungle path. Enjoy the ruins, lagoons, nature treks, kayaking and rock-climbing.

YUCATÁN

Mérida

$ Colonial Hotel

Calle 62 #476 at Calles 57 y 59. 999-923-6444; US Toll-free: 888-886-2982. www.hotelcolonial.com.mx.

73 Mexican-decorated rooms in the historic downtown area. The hotel also has a travel agency, solarium, swimming pool, bar service, parking, and medical service.

$ Luz En Yucatán

Calle 55 #499 at 60 y 58. 999-924-0035. www.luzenyucatan.com.

Fully-furnished studio and one-bedroom en-suite apartments. The pool is in a private, walled garden, while the hotel, three blocks from the plaza, has Wi-Fi internet.

$$ Casa Del Balam Hotel

Calle 60 #488 at Calle 57. US Toll-free: 800-624-8451. www.casadelbalam.com.

This well-known colonial hotel faces the Opera House and University, two blocks from the main plaza. Room service, parking, pool, garden cafe/bar and Restaurant.

$ Hotel Trinidad

Calle 62 #464 at Calle 55, Centro. 999-923-2033. www.hotelestrinidad.com.

Two and a half blocks from Plaza Mayor, this renovated 19 room colonial mansion has something for all tastes and budgets. Facilities include continental breakfast, a new air conditioned games room and wireless internet access.

$ Hotel Trinidad Galeria

Calle 60 at Calle 51, Centro. 999-923-2463. www.hotelestrinidad.com.

This 33 room hotel excites your cultural tastebuds with original works of art virtually everywhere.

$$$ Hyatt Regency Mérida

Calle 60 #344, Paseo Montejo. 999-942-0202; US Toll-free: 800-233-1234. www.hyatt.com.

This familiar base for business trips has 300 rooms and suites near the financial district.

Campeche

$ Villa Uxmal

Km76 Carr. Mérida vía larga. 997-974-6020. www.villas arqueologicas.com.mx.

Two-minute walk from the ruins, this peaceful hacienda-style property has 43 rooms, a large swimming pool and central courtyard amid lush tropical garden.

$$$$ Hacienda Puerta Campeche

Calle 59, No. 71 Pro 16 & 18. 981-816-7535. www.haciendasmexico.com.

15 rooms and suites overlook the swimming pool and gardens at this 17th century colonial

building in the historic city center. The five star hotel is also home to "La Guardia" restaurant. Chef Rafael Esparza blends regional and international cuisine using local, organic ingredients.

Chichén Itzá

$ Villa Chichén Itzá

Km120 Carr. Mérida Valladolid Ap 0495, Chichén Itzá. 985-856-6000. www.villasarqueologicas.com.mx.

Find respite from the ruins (*10min walk*) in these tropical gardens with 43 guestrooms overlooking a pool and accented by Mayan statues. Enjoy the sound and light show at Chichén-Itzá each night!

VALLADOLID

$ El Mesón del Marqués

Calle 39 No. 203, between calles 40 and 42. 985-856-2073. www.mesondelmarques.com.

This hacienda on the north side of Valldolid's main square has aged well, with a picturesque central patio and restaurant seving Yucatán cuisine. Rooms are simple but comfortable.

ISLA HOLBOX

$$$ CasaSandra Hotel

Calle de la Igualdad, Lazaro Cardenas, Isla Holbox. 984-875-2171. www.casasandra.com.

Cozy, boutique hotel with 12 superior rooms and suites facing the beaches of Holbox Island.

RESTAURANTS

Yucatecán cuisine promises far more than just *burritos* (*see below*). Price and quality usually don't equate here. Dining options range from simple *loncherías* (they serve lunch) to cheap *cocinas economicás*, while *restaurantes* vary from tourist traps to traditional havens in beautiful surroundings. *Restaurantes* open early to prepare for the main meal of the day: lunch, eaten at about 2pm (on Sundays followed by a *siesta*). The *cena* (dinner) is a light meal eaten after 9pm. Most Yucatecán restaurants (except Riviera Maya) close at 6–7pm. If you're looking for a snack, just ask for *antojitos*. *Cantinas* (bars) serve Yucatecán-style tapas called *botana*.

Yucatecán Food

Fish and seafood are staples throughout the Yucatán, as are maize, beans, subtle herbs, fresh fruite, lime, cilantro and chilli. Literally anything can and will be served in a tortilla.

Camote – Sweet potato, normally served with coconut.

Candied pumpkin.

Chaya – A sort of tree spinach.

Cochinita Pibil – Suckling pig in a traditional sauce.

Guajolote en salsa negra - Turkey in black sauce.

Joroches – Dumpling stew.

Longaniza – *Chorizo*-style sausage.

Mucbil pollo – Large tamale (*see tamale*) with a chicken, anchiote and chaya (*see chaya*) filling.

Panucho – Small tortilla (*see tortilla*) filled with fried black beans and shredded meat, then fried and topped with more shredded meat.

Papadzule – Warmed tortilla stuffed with hard-boiled eggs and topped with pumpkin seed sauce.

Pimes – A thick tortilla.

Pipián – A sauce made from pumpkin seeds, served over meat.

Pozole – Soup made with mazie, pork and beans.

Puchero – Type of stew.

Pumpkin seed mazapán.

Queso relleno – Cheese with seasoned meat.

Salbute – Small, thick tortilla topped with shredded meat and sauce.

Sopa de lima – Chicken soup with tortilla and lime.

Tamale – Baked corn dough parcel, with or without filling.

Tortilla – Thin unleavened bread.

Yuca – Starchy root vegetable.

Yucatecán Drinks

Unusual local drinks include:

Anise water (aniseed).

Balché – Mead from the bark of a leguminous tree, honey and water.

Corn atole – Spiced, cornstarch-based drink.

Horchata –Vegetable beverage made of ground nuts or seeds.

Xtabentún – Aniseed and honey liqueur.

$	<$10
$$	$10–$20
$$$	$20–$30
$$$$	>$30

CANCÚN

$ El Fish Fritanga

Blvd. Kukulcán, by the police station.

This is your spot for great seafood and prices, plus a lovely view of the lagoon. If you like intrigue, try the shark *tacos* and *empanadas*.

$ Los Huaraches de Alcatraces

Alcatraces #31.
998-884-3918. Tue–Sun.

Enjoy a typical Mexican meal out on the southeast corner of the Parque de las Palapas, or a tasty traditional *antojito*.

$$ Los Almendros

Av. Bonampak at the corner of Sayil, in front of the Plaza de los Toros. 999-922-7844.

Yucatecán homecooking at its finest, with few whistles and bells in a family atmosphere.

$$ Casa Rolandi

Plaza Caracol Shopping Mall, Blvd. Kukulcán Km8.5. 998-883-2557. www.rolandi.com.

Excellent wood-oven pizzas and Italian cuisine.

$$ La Habichuela

Margaritas #25 Downtown, near the Parque de las Palapas. 998-887-1716. www.lahabichuela.com.

An award-winning mainstay of Cancún fine dining with Mayan architecture and tropical gardens. Try the signature *Cocobichuela*—shrimp and lobster in curry sauce, served in a coconut and garnished with tropical fruit.

$$ Labná

Margaritas # 29, near Parque de las Palapas. 998-884-3158. www.labna.com.

High arched ceilings echo this restaurant's namesake. The *comida típica* of the Yucatán served here stands high in its own right.

$$ Pericos

Av. Yaxchilán #61, 998-884-3152. www.pericos.com.mx.

Bring the family for the daily marimba and mariachi performances, and talk over your grilled meats and Mexican fare about the colorful *recuerdos* of the revolution that surround you.

$$$ La Casa del las Margaritas

La Isla Shopping Village, Blvd. Kukulcán Km12.5. 988-883-3222. www.lacasadelasmargaritas.com.

Designed as a "celebration of good taste, good eating and good moments", Casa de las Margaritas is sure to delight you with its festive atmosphere, varied Mexican cuisine and live performances.

$$$ La Madonna

La Isla Shopping Village, Blvd. Kukulcán Km12.5. Noon–midnight daily. 998-882-2222. www.lamadonna.com.mx.

Contemporary chic fine Italian and Swiss dining below the all knowing smile of the Mona Lisa. Full martini bar and excellent service.

ISLA MUJERES

$ Café Cito

Matamoros 42. 998-877-1470.

This bright café and bistro—where your food will be served on a glass bottom table over seashells on a white sand beach—has long been hailed on Isla for its fabulous, even decadent waffles. You can eat breakfast and watch the island life here until 2pm. Come for a light lunch or an icecream cone.

$ Coctelería Justicia Social

Av. Medina across from the Navy Base.

A sure bet for *mariscos*, this simply authentic *coctelería* is run by the local fisherman's co-op, whose members dock at the restaurant to unload their fresh catch.

$ La Lomita

Juárez 25B, two blocks south of the plaza, up the hill.

"The Little Hill" has authentic *comida corrida* at $30 pesos, well worth the hike; the wait among locals is worth the trip on its own.

$$$ Casa O's

South end, on the road to Garrafón. Open daily at 1pm. 998-888-0170.

This is your place for a romantic sunset meal from the sea, looking out on the Caribbean. Leave room for the Key Lime Pie.

$$$ Casa Rolandi's

In the Hotel Villa Rolandi, Carr. Sac Bajo. 998-877-0700.

Casa Rolandi's creative menu is served on a romantic candle-lit terrace overlooking the Caribbean. The gourmet Italian dishes are supurb, and the service is excellent.

COZUMEL AND SOUTH

Cozumel

$ Casa Denis

Calle 1 Sur 132. 987-872-0067. www.casadenis.com.

This Yucatecán restaurant has been running for over 90 years. Be sure to take a look at the history of Cozumel in photos on the walls.

$ Paradise Cafe

Costera Sur Highway, Km 33.

A small palapa restaurant on the windward, eastern coast, just around the southern tip. Has the best conch ceviche anywhere, beer, hammocks and ocean waves.

$ Especias

Calle 3 between 5ta Av. and 10ª Av.

A great spot to enjoy the sunset outside over world cuisine, with seafood, and excellent service.

$ Sabores

5ta Av. between Calles 3&5. A yellow house with a small sign. Lunch daily noon to 4:30pm. No English spoken.

This home and restaurant serves delicious *comida corrida* on its back patio. Ask to peek inside the pots for a sampling of today's menu.

$$ La Choza

Adolfo Rosado Salas 198, at Av.10 Sur. 987-872-0958. www.lachozarestaurant.com.

La Choza serves slow-cooked traditional Yucatecán dishes and fresh seafood beneath its palapa.

$$ Guido's

Av. Rafael Melgar 23. 987-872-0946. www.guidoscozumel.com.

Enjoy a wood oven pizza and a pitcher of fresh sangria inside this colorful Italian joint, or outside on the terrace.

Puerto Morelos

$ Le Cafe D'Amancia

On the zócalo across from the church. Open daily 8am–2pm and 6pm–10pm.

A quiet corner for a chat, email checking, fancy coffee, fresh juices and breakfast delicacies.

$ Hola Asia

On the south side of the zócalo. Open Wed–Mon for 1pm–10pm. 998-871-0679.

Hola Asia has this puerto's best Chinese, Japanese, and Thai cuisine—including sushi—and a fabulous location with a terrace overlooking the sea and the main square.

$ La Petita

One block North from the square on Av. Melgar.

An old favorite for locals and travelers, this is a bustling spot with well prepared fresh seafood and Mexico's characteristic charm.

Playa del Carmen

$ Ah Cacao Chocolate Café

5ta Av. at Constituyentes. 984-803-5748. www.ahcacao.com.

Named for the king of Tikal, this café honors the time old tradition of *cacao* and brings you fine natural ingredients in all their creamy and chocolatey wonder.

$ Babe's

Calle 10 between 5ta Av. and 10ma Av.

Swinging Babe's cooks up Thai noodles, curries, and Swedish meatballs—the Swedish chef's specialty. From the bar try *mojitos* and mango *margaritas*.

$ El Fogón

30a Av. at Calle 4; 30a Av. at Calle 32; Constituyentes near 30a Av.

Come to any of three locales for lots of cheap and delicious food. Local favorites include the *tacos al pastor* and *frijoles charros*.

$ Hot

Calle Corazón at Calle 14.

An old Playa standard for coffee and sweets over the morning paper or casual conversation—not for those who are in a hurry.

$ El Oasis

Calle 12 between 5ta Av. and 10ª Av.

Popular opinion has it that El Oasis serves Playa's best shrimp *tacos*. Also on the menu are many other delights from the sea, and a full bar.

$ La Tarraya

Calle 2 at the sea.

One of Playa's oldest culinary institutions, come sit beachside over delectable seafood plates, or bring your own catch of the day and a recipe you'd like prepared.

$$ La Casa del Agua

5ta Av. near Juárez. 984-803-0232.
www.lacasadelagua.com.

The classy "House of Water" serves international cuisine and seafood in one of three dining areas: the ground floor Bistro, the open air roof garden looking out over the Caribbean Sea, or the main dining room where live music will accompany you on weekend nights.

$$$ Yaxché

Calle 8 between 5ta and
10a Av. 984-873-2502.
www.mayacuisine.com.

This Playa institution is the place to experience Mayan Cuisine—the *mestizaje* of Mayan, Yucatec and European flavors—in decor that embodies the Yucatán. Be sure to follow your dinner with a flaming cup of Mayan coffee prepared at your table, or a glass of *Xtabentun*.

Akumal

$ El Ultimo Maya

Main street West of the highway, in front of the water tower.

It is well worth the walk for this authentic Mayan meal.

$$ La Buena Vida

On the beach at Half Moon Bay. Happy hour 5pm–7pm.

Come for a breakfast, lunch or dinner of classic cuisine and enjoy the many beach activities that surround "The Good Life."
The rooftop swing bar is the best spot for an unforgettable sunset.

$$ La Cueva del Pescador

On the plaza. 984-875-9255.

This festive fisherman's dive will serve up the day's catch on tree trunk tables over a sandy floor. Try the *ceviche de caracol.*

Tulum

$ Don Huacho

Av. Tulum between Beta and Osiris

This local institution is a favorite for seafood and *ceviche.*

$ Hola Primo

On the plaza, two blocks East of Av. Tulum on Acuario.

Local fare and ambience, including excellent empanadas and a gamut of *salsas* for dipping.

$$ Charlie's Restaurant and Art Gallery

Av. Tulum. 984-871-2573.

This restaurant and bar serves up tasty Mexican cuisine in a festive setting, and doubles as a gallery for local artisans. Come for live music and dancing on Saturday nights.

$$$ Hechizo

Tulum Beach Road at Rancho San Eric, Reservations highly advised. 984-100-0710.

The trip south to the entrance to Sian Ka'an is well worth it for the fine dining and international cuisine presented at this small gem.

Cobá

Ruins

The restaurant in the parking lot of the ruins at Cobá serves cheap and delicious Mayan food. On the main drag, try **Restaurant Bocadito ($)** overlooking the lake.

Punta Allen

$ Muelle Viejo

Past the zócalo toward the left along the main pier.

A view of the waterfront, cold beers and tasty seafood dishes.

Chetumal

$$ Las Arracheras de Don José

Corner of Blvd. de la Bahía and Av. OP Blanco

This Uraguayan restaurant, bayside and breezy, is fabulous for dinners of amazing *arracheras*—tender skirt steaks—in *tacos* and *fajitas*.

YUCATÁN AND WEST

Campeche

$ Cenaduría Los Portales

Calle 10 #86, Portales de San Francisco. Dinner only. 981-813-1491.

Campechano home-cooking and local company at outdoor tables beneath the arches of a quiet cobble-stoned colonial square.

$ La Parroquia

Calle 55 between 10 and 12. Open 24hrs. 981-816-8086.

Bustle and chatter, along with traditional cuisine.

$$ Casa Vieja

Calle 10, #319, Upstairs on Los Portales looking over the park. 981-811-1311.

"Old House" serves Cuban cuisine on a second story balcony over-looking the plaza.

$$ La Pigua

Miguel Alemán 179-A. www.lapigua.com.mx. 981-811-3365.

Campeche's legendary seafood restaurant is also classy and bright. You can not go wrong with the coconut shrimp.

Uxmal

$ Chun Yaax Che

Calle 13, # 201, Muna.

Adjoined to the workshop Los Ceibos, the restaurant exhibits the family's work in its gardens and serves local cuisine. It is already widely known for its *pollo pibil* and cooling *piña coladas*.

$ Hacienda Ochil

Km176.5 of the Carr. Mérida–Uxmal. 999-924-7465. www.haciendaochil.com.

The restaurant in the casa grande of remodeled Hacienda Ochil, is a tad less luxurious than its neighbor at **Temozón**, but cooks tasty regional fare in a lovely setting.

$$ Los Almendros

Calle 23 #207, Ticul.

Enjoy the original rural charm of the first of four restaurants renowned for their mastery of traditional Yucatecán *sazón*.

$$ Hacienda Temozón

On the road to Uxmal, turn onto the road to Temozón Sur 5km/3mi, to the Hacienda. www.starwoodhotels.com.

En-route to Uxmal stop in at this stately Hacienda for an elegant breakfast, lunch, or dinner.

Mérida

$ Dulcería y Sorbetería El Colón

Calle 61, North side of the Plaza.

This is the defining dessert spot for Meridianos; do not miss eating a cone on the Plaza!

$$ Villa Maria

Calle 59 at 68. 2pm–midnight daily. 999-923-3357.

Located in a high-ceilinged colonial mansion, Villa Maria has a pleasantly refined ambience and excellent service. Its French Mediterranean menu is also supurb.

$$$ Hacienda Teya

Carr. Mérida–Cancún Km12.5, Kanasín. Noon–6pm. www.haciendateya.com. 999-988-0800.

This stunning 17th century hacienda serves Yucatecán cuisine on stone plates.

$$$ La Pigua

Calle Cúpules 505 at Calle 35. Sun–Tue noon–6pm, Wed–Sat noon–11:30pm. 999-920-3605.

Upscale restaurant serving good Yucatecán seafood dishes.

$$$ Pancho's

Calle 59 #509. 999-923-0942. www.panchosmerida.com.

Historic buildings, contemporary Mexican food, a hopping bar, a garden patio nestled between tropical plants, and fun for all. Music and dancing Wed–Sat after 9pm.

Mérida Backroads

$$$ Casa de Piedra

At Hacienda Xcanatun, Km12 Carr. Mérida-Progreso, 30min drive.

The restaurant at this classy 18C hacienda is located in its renovated machine house, where a grand piano sounds Thu–Sun 2pm–4pm, and high ceilings and a lovely terrace are the setting for scrumptious cuisine.

Izamal

$$ Kinich

Calle 27, between Calles 28 and 30. 988-954-0489. www.sabordeizamal.com.

Named for Izamal's largest remaining pyramid and the god of the sun, Kinich Kakmo restaurant serves rich *comida yucateca* at a decent price.

$$ Macan ché

Calle 22 #305 x 33 &35. Dinner only. 988-954-0287.

A touch of something special dots the Yucatán-influenced international cuisine at Macan che Bed and Breakfast. Be sure to call in your dinner order an hour ahead.

Celestún

 $ La Playita

On the beach in Celestún.

Celestun's oldest seafood joint, is popular among the locals and serves many local specialties in a quaint regional ambience. If your appetite is robust after a day at sea try the *filete relleno*, a stuffed fish fillet that will stuff you too!

$$ La Palapa

On the Beach in Celestún.

This large beachfront restaurant, named for its traditional-style roof, conjures Caribbean excess in size and modernity but also has good seafood and service.

Valladolid

The Bazar Municipal (**$**; *corner of Calles 39 and 40*) has tasty local fare, good for late-night bites.

$ Restaurante San Bernardino de Siena (Don Juanito's)

Calle 49 #227, two blocks from the Convento San Bernadino, 856-2740.

A local favorite for lunch or dinner, serving grilled meats and seafood.

$ Restaurante Zací

Kitchen closes at 6pm sharp.

For a great view and *comida tipica*, come to the restaurant adjoined to the cenote of the same name, two blocks from Valladolid's plaza. Try the sampler for a taste of seven different dishes, then go for a swim; the cenote entrance fee is included with your meal.

$$ Hosteria el Marques

Calle 39 #203. 856-2073.

On a lovely quiet courtyard inside the Hotel Meson del Marques, this fine restaurant has a Yucatecán sampler and other delicious regional dishes.

Isla Holbox

$ La Cueva del Pirata

Main plaza. 984-875-2183.

The Pirate's Cave specializes in Italian fare and seafood and promises a lively ambience.

$$ Faro Viejo

Av. Juárez y Playa.

Enjoy a view of the sunset and sea breeze at this open air seafood restaurant.

Chichén Itzá

$ Try the *loncherias* along the small plaza at the west end of Pisté town for cheap and fast local fare.

$ Las Mestizas

Calle 15 s/n. 985-851-0069.

Along the main road in Pisté, Las Mestizas has regional cuisine, good service, atmosphere and prices.

Progreso

$ Sol y Mar

Calle 19 and 80.

This popular local haunt serves seafood and *botanas* on an open second story terrace overlooking the *malecón*. Live music and lounge chairs.

RESTAURANTS

CANCÚN AND YUCATÁN

INDEX

INDEX